THE REAL LIVES OF STRONG BLACK WOMEN

THE REAL LIVES
OF STRONG
BLACK WOMEN

Transcending Myths, Reclaiming Joy

TOBY THOMPKINS

AGATE

CHICAGO

Printed in Canada.

Thompkins, Toby.
    The real lives of strong black women : transcending myths, reclaiming joy / by Toby Thompkins.
       p.   cm.
    ISBN 1-932841-00-8 (hardcover)
    1. African American women—Social conditions. 2. African American women—Biography. 3. African American women—Life skills guides. I. Title.
    E185.86.T43 2004
    920.72'089'96073—dc22

                             2004016231

10 9 8 7 6 5 4 3 2 1

Agate books are available in bulk at discount prices. For more information, go to agatepublishing.com.

To my mother, the late Anna Mae Thompkins,
and my wonderful father, Nathaniel Thompkins.
Thank you for teaching me that love
is the greatest strength of all.

CONTENTS

FOREWORD BY VICTORIA ROWELL

As black women in America, we all have an innate sense that strength is a part of our ancestral constitution. Our legacy as black women began in Africa and it was built upon a very real strength. Nothing about that legacy is mythical. Strength is the infrastructure of a black woman's life. Whether we flourish or flounder, we call upon that infrastructure of strength in order to traverse the mountains and valleys of our lives. This much I know for sure: black women are wired to be strong.

Our strength has deceived some black men to operate under the assumption that black women should be the quintessential mother/lover. The expectation that all black women should cook, clean, and still be the consummate lover stems from the fact that many black men have grown up in black matriarchal households. In this setting, black women operate as the pillar of strength. This is not a figment of the imagination, because the woman in black American families today is all-powerful. This is certainly my reality, since the black woman who raised me also raised thirteen children. Her strength is the most precious heirloom she passed on to me. I inherited her fierce independence—but there is no doubt it is an independence that bears a great cost! However, my independence offers a freedom that I and other Strong Black Women are not willing to forfeit. Consequently, the stakes are high for black women who *choose* to be independent—who choose to be strong—because they also risk inheriting lives of solitude.

I once dated an NBA player, and during that time I was able to illustrate to him in ample terms the content of my character. One day he turned to me and said, "Vicki, when I am with you I feel like I am in the CBA [Continental Basketball Association—a minor league] and you are in the NBA." On the one hand he was fascinated by my vision, intelligence, and strength; conversely, those same qualities intimidated him. One of the challenges of being Strong Black Women is living the legacy of past strength. Often times, our strength is misinterpreted in mythical terms by those we love and those who want to love us.

As a black woman, a mother, and an advocate for millions of foster children across America, I believe we must call upon our courage to love and to allow joy in our lives no matter what the dictates of our lives might be. Toby Thompkins's book speaks honestly and lovingly to the ways *all* women, and not just black women, must free themselves from the emotional and social traps our lives force upon us. As black women, we walk in a world that provides us very few safety nets. Our gait is purposeful, but that does not mean we wish to walk alone.

I am a single mother of two children. I have worked hard, and those before me worked even harder. Like a phalanx they are with me, they are within me, they *are* me.

Victoria Rowell
Emmy-nominated actress,
The Young and the Restless,
and foster care advocate

THE REAL LIVES OF STRONG BLACK WOMEN

A WORD BEFORE WE START:
ANNA MAE AND ME

THE FIRST STRONG BLACK WOMAN I EVER MET WAS ANNA MAE.
We were introduced early one morning in June of 1961 in the ma-
ternity ward of Wilmington General Hospital. I knew from our
first moment together that this forty-year-old, five-times-married,
oldest daughter of eighteen in a small farming family in northeast
Maryland was indeed a Strong Black Woman. She had arranged
for us to meet in spirit long before that day. After several months of
being bedridden due to a difficult pregnancy and the looming risk
of miscarriage, she did not want to miss a moment of the festivities
surrounding my arrival and our meeting. She was so determined
to have things go her way that she misled the attending nurses
regarding the timing of her contractions so that they wouldn't rush
her into the delivery room and give her a shot of gas to numb the
pain. Mom worked in that hospital as an LPN. She knew of several
newborn babies who had suffered permanent brain damage due
to invasive techniques used in the delivery room at that time. For
many years after, she would say to me, "I wasn't gonna let a little
pain stop me from making sure that you were all right! I didn't
want those doctors using any clamps to pull you out."

From the very beginning, my mother, like many Strong Black
Women I know, often placed the needs of others above her own
safety and comfort. She was more adept at survival than most of
her contemporaries. Like Mom, Strong Black Women are master
jugglers of life's challenges.

How do these women do it all? Well, I can tell you how my mother did it, because I was there to watch her weave her magic into my life and the lives of everybody she touched. She did it through a lot of self-sacrifice. She sacrificed her dream of becoming a professional businesswoman for the role of housewife and mother. She suffered through years of an estranged and guilt-ridden relationship with my sister, her only daughter, who failed to live up to her expectations. She made her own clothes and bought day-old bread so I could take private violin and piano lessons. Looking back, I see the sacrifices she made were not commensurate with the benefits. But my mother, and millions of women of color just like her, found and cultivated her strength through selfless acts of love and protection. While one could say many things about Mom, you could never say she wasn't a Strong Black Woman. This strength was both her virtue and her vice. It wasn't until the very end of her life that she arrived at her ultimate realization: life is less about being strong and more about being happy.

I never knew much about Mom's inner world. She was happily married to my father, husband number five—a loving and devoted man. She never talked much about her previous marriages except to refer to the negative things that had happened. In each situation, there was some straw that broke the camel's back, at which point she left the marriage in an attempt to save her soul and reclaim her happiness. By the time I was born, when she was in her early forties, she had comfortably settled into her role as matriarch: the Strongest Black Woman in our family. Everyone counted on her for every little thing. Very seldom did the phone ring with an offer of comfort or guidance for her, but rather it was usually a request (or a demand) for her strength. She herself never learned how to ask for help when she needed it. Perhaps she gave up hope that anyone else could supply that help for her.

There were many things she kept hidden from the world. For example, I know now that she battled with self-blame, the unhealed hurt of past failed relationships, and the numbing pain of being black and female in America. Her personal struggles at times made her controlling, jealous, obsessive, and insecure.

Her strength came with the expectation that everyone she loved should be perfect, according to her definition. If they failed to live up to her expectations—and they often did—it was as if she had failed herself. She showed her love first through sacrifice, then compassion.

Over the years from childhood to adulthood, I was shaped by that sacrifice, and that strength. She was my Superwoman, my Get Christie Love, my Oh Mighty Isis. In time, I began to see the toll that being everybody's everything was taking on her emotional, spiritual, and physical health. She showed a fierce game face to the world that counted on her, but few people really knew the conversations that were taking place within her, among her head, heart, and soul. It takes a lot out of a woman to live a life in which she is always battle-ready. Being a Strong Black Woman meant that often she was both the soldier and the Red Cross nurse in everyone's life but her own. The biggest lesson she had to learn about being strong didn't come until about a year before she crossed over.

After a life full of caregiving, penny-pinching, and worrying, Mom developed what I refer to as black folks' diseases: high blood pressure, high blood sugar, and a chronic congestive heart condition. Still, in their golden years Mom and Dad found a lot of pleasure in taking the senior citizen center's day trip to the casinos in Atlantic City. Mom loved "workin'" the quarter slot machines. She would play three machines at a time while canvassing the floor to observe others she felt were "ready to dump." On one particular day, she got lucky and hit the jackpot. The bells and lights, the jingle of the coins falling into the metal plate—it all overwhelmed her, causing a mild heart attack. Mom fell to the floor, her quarters, pocketbook, and personal possessions scattering in every direction. Unconscious, she was rushed to the hospital.

Being the tough old lady that she was, Mom survived that attack like she had so many other challenges. But this particular incident changed her life. A few days later, Mom told me that she believed she'd had a near-death experience. The last thing she remembered was carrying the coins in her arms and yelling for

Dad to come help her guard the money she had won. "The next thing I knew, I was floating peacefully, like a feather, and I saw beautiful bright lights," she said. "It was the most peaceful experience of my life. I had no fear, worry, or pain." Fear, worry, and pain were conditions that had come to define much of the quality of her life at that point. "Toby, if this is what heaven is like, then nobody should be afraid to die." In a strange way, this close brush with death completely changed the way she looked at life.

Over the following year, I watched Mom become another woman. Her brush with death altered her very essence. If was as if she had finally figured out the point of her life and was freeing herself from all of the blame and pain that had defined her sense of self for so long. During the last year of her life, we talked openly and honestly for the first time about the things that really mattered. The often judgmental and overprotective tone that had always characterized much of her manner toward me was replaced with a newfound wisdom—that she had done her best to teach me what she knew about life, and that in the end, it was my life to live. I watched her cultivate the forgiveness she needed to end her lifelong strife with my older sister. She even forgave herself once and for all for the marital mistakes she had made.

And I began to see other small but powerful changes. She ended every conversation or visit with everyone by telling them how much she loved them, as if it were going to be her last opportunity to do so. She and Dad decided to give the grandkids their inheritance while they were both alive, so they could be around to see them enjoy it. More than anything else, she never missed a day of her favorite soap opera, and wouldn't answer the phone when *The Young and the Restless* was on TV. She laughed, cried, joked, and loved like never before.

During this final year of life, Mom's spirit seemed to transcend the torment of her rapidly failing physical condition. It was as if the problems in her body no longer mattered. She used to obsess about how her failing health stopped her from doing things that she needed to do (for everybody else). Now, she did what *she* really wanted to do. Thus, she discovered true inner peace for the first time. Watching Mom reach this level of self-acceptance, self-caretaking, self-love, and self-forgiveness was the greatest gift she could have given me. Being strong was no longer at the center of her equation for living. Just being happy was.

What happened during this time was simply a change in her belief system. She changed how she saw herself in relation to her world and to the people who shared it with her. She turned her sensitivity from self-criticism to self-caretaking. She allowed those she loved to find their own ways in life, rather than insist that they follow the path she deemed best for them. She lovingly and gently forgave herself for her own faults, cherished her simple pleasures, and stopped denying her truth to the world. Why did she have to wait until almost the very end to claim this deeper sense of love, self-care, and joy? Wasn't it there for her all along?

Toby Thompkins

INTRODUCTION:
ABOUT THIS BOOK AND HOW IT WORKS

THE BLACK WOMEN WHOSE STORIES AND EXPERIENCES ARE CONtained in this book affirmed something a lot of smart, loving, and successful sisters have been telling me for a while: "Being a Strong Black Woman is killing us softly." Strength has always been a defining character trait for black women. While strong women are not particular to any race or culture of people, the question of strength has always been more of a gender and race mandate than a personal choice for black women. At once criticized and celebrated for their ability to survive the hardships of black life down through the ages, many sisters have been taught that suffering and self-sacrifice are the key ingredients of a strong or "good" woman. They have had to be strong for their children, their men, their parents, and their communities. After all, every Strong Black Woman is taught at some point in her young life, "God bless the child that has its own."

What was missing from that message is the equation for happiness, directions to overcome that which is silently killing the inner lives of many of the black women I talk to today. When I began to look and listen to the black women in my life, it became clear that, while many of them have a lot to offer the world, they were not "getting theirs" in return. Why does someone who is so routinely effective at tending to the needs of everyone else so often fail at tending to her own personal needs for recognition, respect, love, and gratitude?

Let's not be quick to blame the victim. The myth of the Strong Black Woman was invented by America. While many black women continue to be complicit in perpetrating this mythology of strength, the myth was not created by them. Instead, it was created *for* them.

A brief look at the history of slavery points out the necessity for the myth of the Strong Black Woman. Black women ensured the production, nurturing, and exploitation of the strong and vital slave labor pool that our founding fathers counted upon to create this nation. In exchange, they were stripped of their femininity, their husbands, their children, and their humanity. To survive slavery, you *had* to be strong—for yourself and your loved ones. Being strong was the only way to make it through each day. Being strong was the only way to keep on going when the white man had taken everything that ever mattered in your life from you. Being strong was the only way to offer hope to your spouse and children that a better day was coming. Being strong and "good" was the only way you could hold your head up to your Christian God who promised you that one day your pain and suffering would be replaced by joy and happiness. These are the keys to the myth surrounding the Strong Black Woman: salvation follows suffering, strength precedes happiness—or so it would seem.

The truth of the matter is, many Strong Black Women are living incomplete lives. After centuries of being "good women," today's black women finally realize a "good woman" and a "happy woman" are two different species. Being strong is not a guarantee for salvation or happiness, especially in the case of black women.

For one, being everybody's everything is not getting a sister's personal needs met. In writing this book, I interviewed scores of women from all walks of life and from all different backgrounds, including women from Africa and the Caribbean. Many of the women I interviewed spoke about the mythology of strength as a hurdle caused by the ongoing consequences of patriarchy and racism. Joan Morgan, author of *When Chickenheads Come Home to Roost,* said of her retirement from being a Strong Black Woman, "I realize my retirement requires explanation. This is not to be confused with being strong, black, and a woman. I'm still 'alla' that. I draw strength daily from the history of struggle and survival that is a black woman's spiritual legacy. What I kicked to the curb was the years of social conditioning that told me it was my destiny to live my life as BLACKSUPERWOMAN Emeritus. That by the sole virtues of my race and gender I was supposed to be the consummate professional, handle my life crisis, be the dependable rock for every soul who needed me, and, yes—the classic—require less from my lovers than they did from me because, after all, I was a STRONGBLACKWOMAN and they were just ENDANGEREDBLACKMEN."

Myth is created to make the truth about a situation or experience invisible. It is the *myth* of strength, not the reality, that black women and men must rewrite out of their belief systems. This myth has served to deny us our humanity and hide our pain and suffering. Breaking free from the myth of the Strong Black Woman must be a collective black effort. It requires a rewriting of the black belief system that drives our collective consciousness.

We have many belief systems to rewrite in America. First, there is the belief system of White America that continues to take the best of our black talent and resources while diminishing our participation in the full sweep of American life. But even worse is the belief system of Black America that makes it all right for black men to dehumanize their black women while White America watches and says, "See? I told ya so." One recent example of this was a music video awards event; I watched in total shame and dismay while a hip-hop entertainer walked onto the main stage in a pimp costume accompanied by two scantily dressed, "bootylicious sistas" wearing dog collars and leashes. Where was the outrage? Where was the accountability—to his people, to our black women, even to his own mama? What was he thinking? (And I have to ask, what would have happened if he had walked onto that stage with two white girls leashed and collared that way?) The next morning there was no mention of this atrocity in the press, no chat about his behavior on the internet, and no dialogue at the office water cooler about his lack of accountability to black women. It proved to me yet again that to become an object is to lose your humanity, your voice, and your visibility.

Black women in America, and even within Black America, are still suffering from invisibility. They are still subject to the abuses of a mythology that denies them voice, respect, power, and love. This happens at the hands of men of all races, but especially from black men. Why? because we know they are strong enough to take it! After all, who knows a black woman better than a brotha? We know their secret places, hidden desires, hot buttons, and Achilles heels. We know them because they are our first environment. We call them "bitches" to make ourselves feel strong at their expense, to bend their backs and to make them weak. Then we tell them that they are too strong, too hard, too cold, to deserve our love, respect, and tenderness. So we abandon them in every possible way. Meanwhile, too many of our sisters confuse their complicity with this denigration for strength.

Why Am I Writing This Book?

MUCH TO MY SURPRISE, MANY PEOPLE HAVE ASKED ME WHY I WANTED to write this book. Even more asked me why I feel qualified to write a book about Strong Black Women, since I am a black man. Well, I will answer the second question first. I am the child of a Strong Black Woman. I was raised and shaped by a host of relatives who were also Strong Black Women, and Strong Black Men as well. In accordance with my history, many of my friends are Strong Black People. Finally, for twenty years I have worked as a human relations/cultural diversity consultant for domestic and international corporations that employ women and men of all hues, nationalities, and backgrounds. As I learned from the writings of Dr. Martin Luther King Jr., we are all part of an "inescapable web of mutuality." So, why shouldn't I write about Strong Black Women, or anybody else?

I believe greater levels of self-realization are available for all women and men, strong or otherwise. We can all learn when we stop to analyze the trap of strength—of attempting to be strong to the exclusion of self-realization. In the end, people remember the sum total of your being. Yes, life in Black America is still tough, and racism and sexism will still make sisters and brothers fighting strong. I know because I am a Strong Black Man. But if you dare to sacrifice your chance for true happiness, then you will miss the greatest gift and highest purpose of this journey. As the stories and exercises shared in this book will reveal, the roots of your happiness lie in one place: *your willingness to honor what you believe you owe yourself in this life.*

How Did I Write This Book?

I BEGAN WORK ON THIS BOOK IN THE SUMMER OF 2002 AFTER AN inspiring conversation over a cup of tea with my dear friend Rosie Gordon Wallace. At this time in my life I was still healing from the loss of my mother and examining the greater purpose of my life and career. During our conversation, Rosie challenged me to examine and write about the struggles that many of the women I knew (not unlike my mother) experienced as black women, wives, daughters, and businesswomen. She thought that my background as a life coach to executives and as a consultant in cultural diversity and organizational development, supported by my sensitivity to and appreciation for the unique challenges and contributions of Strong Black Women, would help me write a book from a male perspective that celebrated strength in black women's lives. Since I already knew that black women in America were for the most part misunderstood and undercelebrated, it seemed like a great idea to write a book that celebrated their strength. Initially, I spoke to many black women I knew personally, and they were more than thrilled that I would undertake such an endeavor. But the tone changed when I began to speak with black women whom I didn't know personally. These women began to tell me that being strong created "issues" for them that ultimately were kept alive through myths and stereotypes. They were more interested in my uncovering these myths and stereotypes and the impact they have on the lives of black women who live with them.

I immediately changed the focus of the book project and rewrote the interview questionnaire I'd developed so that I could investigate the costs of being strong in the lives of black women.

During this phase of the project, I conducted approximately fifteen face-to-face one-hour interviews with different women in order to gain a deeper understanding of the role of strength in their lives. I also formed a core group of six special Strong Black Women who read early versions of this book and offered me critical and constructive feedback regarding its form and function.

In total, I collected data from 130 women and 20 men, using both ninety-minute focus-group sessions and hour-long one-on-one interviews, by phone or in person, over a twelve-month period from the fall of 2002 to the winter of 2003. I conducted focus groups in New York, Florida, Illinois, and Philadelphia. In addition, I conducted telephone interviews with men and women from California, Houston, Atlanta, Massachusetts, London, Italy, Bermuda, Jamaica, Cuba, the Dominican Republic, and Switzerland. I reached out to these women and men through a variety of different means: website message boards, www.craigslist.org, internet chat rooms, flyers posted at cafes, and personal referrals. I also invited a list of black women who attended the Harlem Book Fair to participate or to recommend other women and men to participate in a focus group or interview.

The only prerequisite for a woman to participate in my data collection process was that she had to identify herself as a "Strong Black Woman" or "Strong Woman of Color." The women came from very broad and diverse backgrounds in terms of age (from twenty-two to eighty-nine), education (from a high school dropout to a Harvard MBA), class, nationality, and socioeconomic status (from a low-income single mother to a single senior manager in a Europe-based cosmetics company). Likewise, the twenty men I interviewed for this book are just as diverse, and all characterized themselves as having active personal relationships of a romantic or platonic nature with women who they clearly identified as "Strong Black Women" or "Strong Women of Color."

All of the focus-group sessions and most of the one-on-one interview meetings were audiotaped. To ensure confidentiality without compromising the integrity of the data, I changed the names and, in many cases, the geographic background of individuals in order to protect their identities. The only exceptions are in chapters eight and ten, where the names and locations of the women of LIFFT, Rosie Gordon Wallace, Leslie Brown, Megan Kirksey, Bishop Ernestine Reems, and Ellie Jones, are accurate.

An Invitation

I AM INVITING BLACK WOMEN AND MEN TO REWRITE THEIR BELIEF systems. The stories shared in this book will help you identify the myths that usurp your personal power; they will move you further in the direction of your self-realization and happiness; and they will help you cultivate a new kind of self-caretaking. Each chapter of this book concludes with an affirmation statement. Repeat these affirmations to yourself every day. Seize every opportunity to honor the affirmations in your life. They are designed to remind you that you can reclaim more love, more care, and—yes—more joy in your life by setting aside this time for yourself.

While it may be a hundred lifetimes before we change the minds and hearts of all men and women, we can change *our* hearts and minds today. By doing so, you (and I) can challenge the beliefs and alter the lives of the black women and men we love. We can create a self-realized black voice. We can instill deeper love and respect in our intimate relationships. And we can affirm our humanity. Then the myths, the lies, and the stereotypes that haunt us will die. I know this can happen because the story I've shared with you about my mother, Anna Mae, was the story of how one woman, strong and black, changed my life. I hope that this book will inspire you to make this profound shift toward greater joy in your own life.

1 PERFECT LOVE

Above all clothe yourself with love, which binds
everything together in perfect harmony. Colossians 3:14

As far as I can see, many of my sisters are still looking for that big-rock, white-horse, hideaway-mansion, Hollywood kind of love. As a result, many of them still have a lot of unanswered questions about the deeper intricacies of love. A dear friend of mine, who is a beautiful and talented Strong Black Woman, asked me every two weeks for an entire year if I thought her boyfriend of many years still loved her. It was obvious the question of love was always on her mind and was complicated by any number of conditions and forces outside her control. It also occurred to me that no matter how *strongly* you love your man, your fancy job, or your Manolo Blahniks, experiencing perfect love is our greatest challenge.

The black women I interviewed identified three different types of love that take shape in their lives: romantic love, platonic love, and self-love. The order in which they placed these is as significant as the actual types themselves. Most of the women whose stories I share in this book have shifted from ranking romantic love first, then platonic and self-love, to the reverse: first self-love, then platonic love and romantic love. As I listened to these women share their thoughts on love and relationships, three unique (and sometimes nagging) questions emerged regarding the different types of love they experience:

ROMANTIC LOVE	PLATONIC LOVE	SELF-LOVE
Do I deserve your love?	*Do you deserve my love?*	*Do I deserve my love?*

You know the old saying, "It is easier to see in others what you cannot see in yourself"? It should be no surprise that the most examined types of love (romantic and platonic) are experienced outside of ourselves, with other people. Perhaps this is why the women I spoke with were initially more comfortable with enhancing their romantic and platonic relationships than with developing a greater capacity for self-love. Consistently, though, they told me that their journeys to greater happiness and fulfillment challenged them to free themselves from the expectations of having to be everybody's everything. They had to learn how to embrace new and sometimes radical "self-caretaking" behaviors that allowed them to move their lives steadfastly in the direction of their personal joy.

These three forms of love share several important properties that make love the desirable, necessary ingredient for healthy and happy life that it is. These properties are important to every manifestation of romantic, platonic, and self-love. Both black women and black men use these properties to assess the quality and value of all of their loving relationships.

Sustainability

DO YOU WANT A LOVE THAT WITHSTANDS THE TEST OF TIME? SUStainable love is the ultimate test of strength for many women and men. As one sister told me, "The ultimate test of strength in a black woman's life is her ability to get her man and keep her man." How sustainable is the love you are giving and receiving in your life? Do you trust it to always be there? Do you constantly worry that tomorrow the love you give or receive might go away? The value of a deeper self-love is that it increases over time, colored by the high notes and low notes that define all relationships.

The 1990s TV comedy show *In Living Color* featured a regular skit where an older African American couple would argue, and then each would complain to the audience about the difficulties of living with the other. In every skit, one character—usually the wife—would devise newfangled, sinister antics to torture and humiliate her unassuming husband. Appearing to be none the wiser, at the end of the skit, the husband and wife would hold each other in an affectionate embrace and lovingly declare to the folks watching in TV land, "And we're still together!"

Even the platonic bonds of brotherhood and sisterhood are expected to outlast the rivalry and other difficulties that occur between siblings. How many times have you stood in defense of your "low-down, dirty" brother when his girlfriend attempted to trash him in your presence? Even though he may have done her wrong, he is still your brother and your love for him is expected to survive his silly ways. *You* can talk bad about your brother, but you're not gonna stand here and let anyone else talk bad about him in front of your face!

For many black women, being strong means being there through thick or thin, even if they don't get the same treatment from their loved ones in return. Because many Strong Black Women have been conditioned to put up with a lot of silliness and drama in their relationships, they often don't allow themselves the self-love they deserve, desire, and are entitled to enjoy.

Intimacy

WE ALL CRAVE INTIMACY, TO LOVE AND BE LOVED IN THAT PERSONAL, private, completely open way. Yet many of the sisters I spoke to experience a lot of isolation and alienation in their romantic and platonic relationships. Intimacy is a natural and healthy human condition that promotes physical and emotional well-being. Black women and their men need to learn how to overcome our self-imposed barriers to intimacy. We are taught how to give and receive love through the intimacy lessons of our childhood and formative years, particularly through observing our parents. However, sometimes these lessons result in bad emotional patterns when they are shaped by social forces such as racism, sexism, homophobia, and internalized oppression. Unless we make a concerted effort to unlearn negative patterns resulting from those lessons, we pass them on to future generations.

Like so many women, Janet, a newly married, twenty-five-year-old, Afro-Cuban woman, learned how to cultivate intimacy with her spouse through watching positive interactions between her mother and father. "My father worked with his hands and had long, grueling days. His one pleasure in life was a good home-cooked meal, and his favorite was breakfast. Every morning my mother would get up at 5:00 a.m., before my father went to work, and fix him a wonderful breakfast. She said it was her way of showing him how much she cared. My father would bring home a dozen flowers every Friday and give them to my mom. He was a man of few words, but we knew he loved us. They had a very intimate relationship that was less about words and more about symbols.

"I find now that I like doing things for my husband. Just like my mom, it is the little things that I do to show him how much I love him. Mom used to place one single stem in a vase every morning and set it next to his café con leche on the breakfast table. It was like a symbol of her love for him. They taught me that loving actions really speak louder than lovely words."

While stylish luggage becomes the sophisticated traveler, excessive personal baggage can cause the death of intimacy in any relationship. Some strong sisters carry their baggage from relationship to relationship like they are going on an around-the-world cruise. Being strong for everybody else often means that you are constantly relieving others of their baggage. Consequently, many Strong Black Women seldom have room in their baggage for their own stuff. They don't take the time to clean out their own suitcases. Even worse, I know Strong Black Women who will take the emotional turmoil of their loved ones and place it into their own baggage, as if to say, "Here baby, let me take that. It's too heavy for you to carry." This kind of strength behavior is also referred to as "dysfunctional rescuing." Black women who inappropriately rescue their loved ones from their uncomfortable or challenging experiences rob those loved ones of their opportunity to experience personal responsibility. This is potentially disabling for the loved ones, since they never learn to lie in the bed that they made. Black women who practice dysfunctional rescuing are often motivated by a hidden agenda: the unhealthy compulsion to feel important or desired. Many will do this even if they must sacrifice their own self-care in the process.

Lois, a college-educated young professional woman who was raised in a low-income household in Chicago, recognized that she had begun to develop a history of dysfunctional rescuing in her relationship with her younger sister. "My baby sister only speaks to me when she needs help paying her rent or she needs a babysitter for her three kids," Lois said. "She never has enough money or time, and she thinks the world owes her a living. I am the first in my family to go to college, and I sometimes feel guilty about that. Now I am slowly realizing that my siblings chose a different path for their lives than I did, but we all had the same opportunities. I have to stop taking care of her or else she will never learn to take care of herself."

Truth-Telling

EVERYONE LOVES A GOOD LIE. WE LIE TO MAKE OUR LOVED ONES FEEL good. We lie to make our loved ones feel bad. And we lie to ourselves more than we lie to our loved ones. Why do we lie so much?

I remember once, when I was still in college, I told a lie about a close female friend that cost me our friendship. She was a sweet, young, and beautiful sister who every brother on campus wanted the chance to date. One year we were in the same study group and became good friends. My fraternity brothers would routinely ask me if I had "tapped dat," to which my honest response was, "No, we're just friends." In time, the pressure from my fraternity brothers intensified. The more time I spent in public with this sister, the more they expected me to get her to "throw down." After several months of harassment regarding my "obligation" to the brotherhood to maintain our reputation as ladies' men, I coughed up the lie they had all been waiting for. I told one person, whom I swore to secrecy, that I had "kicked it" with this young sister. I also told him that it was just a one-time thing and not to make too much of it. As you might imagine, news of my alleged score spread across the campus like wildfire, and before I knew it, my friendship with this lovely woman was over. To this day I sincerely regret ever having told this lie.

Lies protect myths. They imprison the truth and turn us away from love and self-respect. Most importantly, lies always come to light, and when they do, somebody (very often somebody we love) always gets hurt. I am probably not telling you anything that you don't already know, but why do we continue to avoid truth-telling in our relationships? The answer is simple—fear.

When Strong Black Women talked to me about their challenges with truth-telling, they rattled off a long list of fears that drove them to lying. Fear of rejection, fear of success, fear of failure, fear of intimacy, and fear of abandonment topped their lists. When we fear something, we don't think we have power over it; in fact, we think it has power over us. I believe our fear of truth-telling stems from our difficulty finding *constructive* ways to tell the truth.

Marianne Williamson, a minister and author of *A Return to Love,* came to my church and made a very powerful point about truth-telling: "Honesty without compassion is brutality." We need to learn more effective ways to tell the truth, even when what the world wants is a lie. We need to learn more sensitive ways to tell the truth in a manner that protects the dignity and self-respect of our loved ones, but doesn't allow them to keep operating from myth or social pressure. Only when we learn to tell the truth, the right way, all of the time, will we open ourselves to a deeper experience of love and self-caretaking.

These three properties—sustainability, intimacy, and truth-telling—are essential to every kind of love. Now, let's take a look at the three different types of love that are shaped in the lives of black women and men.

Romantic Love: Do I Deserve Your Love?

BLACK WOMEN IN AMERICA HAVE INHERITED A HISTORY THAT SAW their husbands castrated and lynched before their eyes, and their children snatched from their loving arms and sold into slavery.

It is no small wonder that many black women are nervous about trusting the sustainability of the romantic love that comes into their lives. History helped teach black women that their black men wouldn't be around long. They were taught they would have to go through life on their own so they should learn to be strong, stand on their own two feet, and get used to being alone. They were taught that being strong was about survival, and there was little if any place for love in their lives. Letting go of those generations of hard lessons and memories is no small feat. Doing so requires the strength to move beyond the imprinting of racism and sexism that defines what "true love" is, and what kind of love black women should be willing to accept.

Most importantly, doing so requires a black woman to move away from an oppressive, emotionally frozen independence that espouses crazy superwoman logic like, "I don't need anyone, I can do it all by my damn self." Doing it by your damn self might make you strong, but it sure doesn't guarantee your happiness. (And by the way, it excuses the rest of the world from contributing to *the happiness you deserve.*) If we were born to go through life all by ourselves, then we would still be simple one-cell organisms. Life and love happen as a result of our ability to divide and multiply ourselves. Out of this process, we heal, learn, laugh, grow and love. Do ya feel me?

Lessons from down through the ages about what kind of love black women can expect from black men color their belief that black men are for the most part commitment-phobic. Consequently, some black women I talked with feel they must cajole or even trick their men into making a commitment. In this case, commitment is a metaphor for monogamy, but in practice it is much more. Let me ask you a question. Would you eat a cake that was only half-baked? Of course not. Then why would you give your heart, soul, and body to someone who wasn't ready to handle them with the utmost care and compassion? This kind of logic entraps the hunter, not the prey. While many sisters are hunting for the right love, is it really worth setting yourself up as the bait in your own defective trap? I have seen the hearts of several women rot under these circumstances. Even if the man you capture becomes commitment-ready, it doesn't necessarily mean he will make the ultimate commitment to you. So what's a sister to do?

Before you give up altogether on trying to figure out the true intentions of black men in love, please know that a lot of black men truly believe in the idea of love. They also believe in the idea of committed romantic relationships, even if they don't entirely trust them in practice. As a result of this mistrust, many black men have learned to separate love and sex (a distinction that causes a lot of hurt and frustration for women everywhere). Even so, I hear a lot of brothers talk about the type of sister with whom they hope to one day settle down and build a life. More than anything, they want to be able to let their guards down in their romantic relationships—in essence, to be honest and vulnerable. So beware: kick your man while he is naked and in love with you, and he will leave you faster than you can say "see ya!"

Now, I will acknowledge that a number of women I have spoken to about this totally disagree with me, but remember that black women aren't the only members of our race who have been emotionally and psychically scarred by our American legacy. Black men have deeply rooted psychic and emotional wounds that they need to heal as well. Even with all the progress black men have made since slavery, and the unearned privilege that we possess as men in a man's world, we are still a deeply wounded people.

Unfortunately, black women too often are subject to black men's pain as well. Too often they have suffered rejection, ridicule, and abuse from black men in response to their attempts to show them a deeper love. But don't interpret our acting out as a lack of capacity for love, intimacy, and commitment. In many ways, it is a cry for help, because black men still haven't totally embraced our own need for greater self-love. Not even black women are strong enough to heal all of us. *You* aren't strong enough to do our healing work for us. Just allow us to do what we must do for ourselves. Some of us will embrace our healing process sooner than others. When you see a black man who has embraced his right to heal himself, you will have met a black man who is ready, willing, and able to commit to a loving relationship.

A lot of black women still try to change black men. Many fear the possibility they might give their love to white women or to other men. If that is the journey that a black man must take to arrive at a place of his own healing and self-love, let him be about his business. Don't judge him, don't chase after him, and don't hate him. No matter what, he is still your brother, and he still loves and needs you as his ally. Just respectfully invite him to move out of the way, because the right man for you is standing behind him and trying to get through.

Before we move on to platonic love, take a moment to think about the behaviors and attitudes you possess that are delaying you from receiving the love you desire. Now finish this statement before we move forward:

"To stay open to receiving the love I deserve, I will
_____."*

Platonic Love: Do You Deserve My Love?

PLATONIC LOVE IS THE LOVE WE SHARE WITH MOST OF THE PEOPLE in our lives, love involving friendship or affection without sexual relations. Platonic love can be just as complicated as romantic love. We play multiple roles in our lives through which we have the opportunity to cultivate platonic love relationships. Our family roles as parent, child, sibling, cousin, and so on are supported by the social expectation that we should strive to love all descendants of our bloodline. As a result, we are more embracing and more forgiving of relatives because, after all, blood is thicker than water, right?

Cultivating platonic friendships presents different challenges. Most friendships are built around shared core values. Since we prize these core values within ourselves, they serve as the soil that nourishes our loving platonic relationships with others. Unfortunately, our conditioning about cultural differences like race, gender, religion, physical ability, age, and sexual orientation can stop or delay us from getting to the core values we share with others. However, I for one have observed that each new generation has a greater ability to jump those hurdles and embrace loving platonic relationships with people who look, act and experience the world differently than they do. This trend gives me hope.

When love and sex are part of a relationship, we say we have fallen "in love." When we fall in love, it is as if we have transcended our separateness to create a new, shared identity; our essence is redesigned to incorporate qualities, values, and behaviors that didn't exist when we were alone and not in love. The shared values feel richer to us. This experience for most women and men is simply intoxicating. In platonic relationships where love grows without sex, we can still experience an intoxicating union with someone else. This intoxication is based on a simpatico feeling between the people forming the relationship. Sympathy, compatibility, and companionship are key ingredients in creating a high-quality platonic love relationship. Even if sexual chemistry is present for one or both members of a platonic relationship, acting on it changes the very nature of the relationship.

Black women who live under the myth of strength sometimes find it difficult to ask for or cultivate mutual experiences of sympathy, compatibility, and companionship in their loving relationships. To do so can be misconstrued as a sign of weakness. The platonic roles they play in life—as boss, parent, co-worker, neighbor, child, friend, and sibling—represent unique challenges for black women. These are the very roles through which their strength is displayed and evaluated by society. As such, this is where black women also battle or succumb to the Strong Black Woman myth that robs them of more emotionally balanced relationships with their loved ones. As mythical women, they don't require the same space for human error or sensitivity as the rest of us. They can handle their own drama, endure more pain, take on more of life's daily pressures, and never let you see them sweat. They don't leave any room to cultivate or embrace the love, self-care, and joy they need in their lives.

In episode after episode in the life of the mythical Strong Black Woman, she must appear ready to do battle. She must protect her weaker loved ones and make sure that everyone feels safe and secure. She often feels guilty at the thought of calling on loved ones for support. No matter how strong they appear to be, sisters need to be able to count on the strength of their loved ones, too. Sometimes they become so vested in the myth that they don't know how to ask for help until it is too late. Strong Black Women deserve the same level of love and consideration that they endlessly supply to others. When they don't learn how to ask for support, comfort, and understanding in their platonic relationships, those relationships become one-sided.

When this happens, these women become what I call "chronic caregivers," a common experience for many women of color. Such was the case for Linda, a twenty-eight-year-old chronic caregiver who finally learned how to set healthy boundaries and create more balance in her roles as daughter and sister.

Linda grew up in a small town in southern New Jersey. She lived in this little town all her life and often dreamed of leaving to work in another country. She was single and had a great job at the corporate office of a multinational company that was headquartered just a few towns over. Linda had two older brothers who both got married and moved away, leaving her to take care of her aging parents. However, her brothers still lived within twenty minutes of her hometown.

Linda was very active in the community and taught Sunday school at the church she attended as a child. Life for Linda was full, but still unfulfilling. "It seems that I never got any time to myself to go someplace new or meet new people," she said. "I didn't really mind taking care of my parents; after all, they were great parents. Since I am single I had more time to devote to them. It was all part of being a good daughter, I guess. Things will change once I marry, but first I had to find the time to go on a date."

To begin to address what was missing in her life, Linda signed up for an introductory dating service, where she met Donald, an investment banker who lived in New York City. At first, her friends and relatives seemed happy that she had met a nice guy. But that didn't last long. "After about two months of dating Donald, I wanted to start spending more time in New York City. Donald had really interesting friends, and I loved the New York

City nightlife. So I asked my brothers to share in caregiving for my parents on the weekends so I could have some time to spend with Donald.

"I was so surprised when my brothers refused to step up to the plate and give me some free time on my weekends. They had never lifted a finger before to care for my parents, but were first to the door when my parents wanted to give away some old family antiques. I never complained about it in the past, but the more I thought about it, the more I realized they had been letting me carry the load for years and never even offered a word of appreciation.

"After several very heated arguments, I got the attention and support of both of my sisters-in-law. A short time later, my brothers decided it would be a good thing for their children and their parents to spend more time together. They agreed to come and get Mom and Dad for visits with their grandkids on the weekends I was out of town.

"I was sorry I had to put my foot down, but I am glad it all worked out. It made me realize how much of a chronic caregiver I had become. I should have taken time for myself long before I started dating Donald. I felt a lot of guilt in even asking my brothers to help because I didn't want my parents to get the wrong idea. But in the final analysis, I had to stop being such a Strong Black Woman and carve out some 'me' time."

Self-Love: Do I Deserve My Love?

LOVING OURSELVES IS THE FIRST AND ONLY PATH TO CREATING *GOOD lovin'* in all other relationships. *Self-love* is the personal commitment to slowing down enough to embrace stillness, healing, and renewal as a daily part of your own life. It also means nurturing and enriching every part of the self: mind, body, and spirit. *Self-caretaking* is how you embrace and incorporate the care of the mind, body, and spirit into your being and daily life ritual. Self-caretaking is created twice, first on the inside and then on the outside.

I grew up dancing to the soul-stirring songs of the Jackson

Five. One of my favorites was "The Love You Save." It's only now that I truly understand the power behind this song's chorus: "Stop! The love you save may be your own. Darlin' take it slow, or someday you'll be all alone." Slowing down enough in life to love yourself is one of the most daunting challenges we face. It has only been in recent years that the workplace has begun to make the connection between self-care, employee satisfaction, and sustainable performance. Work/life balance programs now teach employees from all walks of life everything from time management to yoga. Learning how to be more gentle and nurturing *regarding your self* enables you to be healthier, happier, and more productive over the long run, in the workplace and in your daily life. This is a foreign concept for too many of today's Strong Black Women.

My mother (like so many, I'm sure) spent long, intense days doing housework for white middle-class families, only to come home and care for her own family with little or no support. Where was the time these women had to take care of themselves when they were so busy providing for everyone else? Where was the time for them to be self-nurturing when their children sucked out of them what little tenderness that remained after catering to the folks in the big house? This is the history of many black women and men. It continues to shape us in more ways than we care to examine.

Do you continue to hear a voice inside of your head telling you that taking care of yourself is for "them," not for you? Do you continue to hear that voice telling you that you have to be strong because the world is against you and counting on you to fail? Do you hear that voice telling you that one day, God will send you somebody who will love you more than you love yourself?

Well, show me the place in the Bible (or any other spiritual text) where God explicitly states that black women do not deserve the same level of love and tenderness that has been bestowed upon women and men of other races and nationalities. Self-love and self-caretaking are not race-based privileges. I believe that self-love is a basic human right, because it is the only path to self-realization. I further believe that self-realization (to become our best, most fulfilled, and most loving selves) is our ultimate goal as human beings. Self-love yields self-caretaking, which in turn yields self-realization. Got it?

Let's not forget that the myth of the Strong Black Woman was created in America. In this society we call free, the only freedom that black women ever had to be kinder and gentler to themselves was realized by their own struggle. Their black men didn't create it for them; nor has White America wholeheartedly come out in support of a black female agenda.

Self-caretaking, for Strong Black Women in particular and all women in general, is a revolutionary act whose time has come. I believe that continuing to create more emotional, spiritual, social, financial, and political freedoms for black women will ultimately transform the world they have historically carried upon their shoulders. To do so, they must continue to embrace self-love through self-caretaking. They must release themselves from the "I can do it by my damn self" form of thinking and move toward a caretaking that is born of love, sisterhood, and fuller participation in the human family.

To create more love in your life, you must know what it feels like when you are getting and giving good lovin'. That is one of the primary goals of this book: to help you understand good lovin' in all its varieties. To begin, you must put self-love first. How do you know when you love yourself? You must look within, and examine those same traits and behaviors that you assess in others to determine the degree to which they love you.

The Love Pie

THE FOLLOWING PASSAGE AND ACCOMPANYING QUESTIONS ARE DESIGNED to help you look more closely at the love you are experiencing in your life. Take some time to meditate on each question. Feel free to discuss these questions with your sister friends and male friends. There are no wrong answers—just unexplored possibilities. By thinking about and answering these questions, you will prepare yourself to explore some of the topics covered in the following chapters with greater insight.

Let's start by thinking about how love is showing up in your life. Imagine the love you experience in your life as a pie cut into three slices. Each slice will represent one of the three main types of love relationships: romantic love, platonic love and self-love. The size of each slice should be based on the degree of personal satisfaction and inner joy you are experiencing in each area of your life. You can even try drawing an actual circle sliced intro three sections, to represent the three kinds of love in your life and how much of each you feel you have. Then answer the questions below.

1. How do you feel about the degree of satisfaction and joy you are experiencing in each slice of your love pie?

2. What are the three main messages or lessons you learned while growing up about romantic, platonic, and self-love that influence how you behave in relation to each slice of your love pie today?

3. Which slice of your love pie has the greatest influence over the other slices and why?

4. What behaviors, attitudes, and habits do you think you can change in order to experience greater satisfaction and joy in your love relationships? Would now be a good time to make those changes in your life? If yes, why? If no, why not, and when would be a good time?

5. How would a redrawn love pie show how your slices would change in size if you made the changes in your life that you identified in the above question?

Before moving to the next chapter, ask yourself:

> *What behaviors, skills, strategies, or attitudes*
> *did I learn in this chapter that can help me*
> *to close the gap between the love pie I am living*
> *and the love pie I want to create in my life?*

Creating a life that is richer in love, joy, and satisfaction starts with understanding the things we do to deny ourselves the love we desire and deserve. The pies you created today can change today if *you* are willing to change. While it may sound simple, it is never that easy. The first step is to make the inner changes by examining the role that self-caretaking plays in how we build our love relationships.

Each remaining chapter in this book will be identified by a corresponding slice or slices of the love pie. That means that the content of a given chapter will support you in your examination of romantic, platonic, or self-love. Some chapters may only address one slice, while others may address issues relevant to multiple slices of your love pie. I recommend reading each chapter consecutively. Pay particular attention to the chapters that speak to those slices for which you are ready to create more love, self-care, and joy in your life.

AFFIRMATION

*Today is all about good lovin'.
I will only give good lovin' to the world and
I will only accept good lovin' in return.*

2 I AM NOT YOUR WONDER WOMAN
(SELF-LOVE)

SEEKING EXTRAORDINARY WOMEN
FOR HIGH-FLYING CAREER OPPORTUNITY

- Are you able to juggle a million and one priorities?
- Do you enjoy carrying the weight of the world on your shoulders?
- Would you like a career where you can be on call twenty-four hours a day, seven days a week, with no overtime compensation?
- Do you possess endless energy and nerves of steel?

If you can answer yes to all of the above, then we want you!

We offer minimal gratitude, a substandard benefit package, sleepless nights, and a lot of other people's thankless problems for you to worry about.

WOMEN OF COLOR are strongly encouraged to apply.

WOULD YOU APPLY FOR THIS JOB? YOU MIGHT IF YOU THOUGHT you were Wonder Woman. I finally got it that Wonder Woman was not just a cartoon—she was a myth. A myth, according to *Webster's,* is "a half-truth that forms part of an ideology about a person, place, or thing." So let's take a look at the so-called truth about Wonder Woman. It is true that she was as strong as any sister from my old neighborhood, but she was also endowed with special powers. For starters, she was white, and being white still counts for a lot of power and unearned privilege in the United States of America. Meanwhile, most of the wannabe Wonder Women in my life are black. Another truth: Wonder Woman never cried, slept, ate, caught a cold, or used the bathroom. Finally, she only had to fight evil and protect the innocent for thirty minutes each week on television. I know sisters who feel they have to kick butt and take names every minute of every day of their lives.

Most importantly, Wonder Woman lived from her truth and to the truth in others' lives. She wore that fabulous gold truth rope that she attached to her side to keep herself safe. When you got in her way, she would wrap her truth rope around you and make you deal with her from your highest and most truthful self. That was her real power. Fortunately, we normal humans have the same power, regardless of our race or gender.

While black people may not come equipped with their very own truth ropes, they do have the power to discern the truth. If this is the case, then why do so many black women still want to be Wonder Women? The truth is that they don't necessarily want to live by that myth any longer, but they don't know how to free themselves of it. As one sister said to me, "I don't want to walk on water, but if I don't, who will do it for me? The problem with being Wonder Women is we work alone. It would be nice if all of the Wonder Women and Men I know could get together in support of each other. You know, like a League of Wonderful Black People. That way we could take turns supporting each other and take a break every now and then."

We are a people of myth and folklore. We were raised on stories that gave us identity, strength, inspiration, and pride. Myth also became a powerful vehicle we used to navigate the hills and valleys of black life in America. Unfortunately, myths—and stereotypes—have also become effective weapons of this country's race-based power system. It's the very system that impedes black women and men from building healthier, more fulfilling lives. Such is the case with the myth of the Strong Black Woman.

In her book, *Saints, Sinners, Saviors: Strong Black Women*

in African American Literature, Trudier Harris, professor of English at the University of North Carolina, writes in detail about the trials and tribulations of the one-dimensional Strong Black Woman: "These suprahuman female characters have been denied the luxuries of failure, nervous breakdowns, leisured existences, or anything else that would suggest that they are complex, multidimensional characters. Black female characters have so frequently been called upon to be strong that strength has repeatedly overshadowed their tenderness, overshadowed their softness, overshadowed the complexity of their femininity and humanity. Indeed, one of the criticisms leveled against the ones who still operate in the human realm is that their strength has crippled black men. What they do—or do not do—to men pales, however, in comparison to what they do to themselves. With strength as their primary trait, they exist in isolated, unchallenged realms of authority where their morality and physical prowess are all they have to comfort themselves."

Black women and men together must still fight against the longstanding threat these myths, stereotypes, and other misrepresentations pose to our well-being. By harnessing our collective power, we can create a way to free ourselves of the myths that continue to define and limit our participation in American society. Overcoming the myth of strength does not mean backing away from the true inner strength that has carried us this far. It means releasing unhealthy, myth-induced attitudes, behaviors, and fears. By freeing ourselves from these, black women and men will make a major leap forward in their individual and collective journeys toward self-realization. We will also upset a power-sharing system built upon myths and lies designed to support the unjust social structure of American life.

As you can see in the diagram below, mythology and negative stereotypes about black people support a system of social power in America that is defined and controlled by human traits that include race, color, nationality, gender, sexual orientation, physical ability, and appearance.

```
┌─────────────────────────────────────────────────────────┐
│  ┌───────────────────────────────────────────────────┐  │
│  │        THE AMERICAN PRIVILEGE PYRAMID             │  │
│  └───────────────────────────────────────────────────┘  │
│  ┌───────────────────────────────────────────────────┐  │
│  │  Unearned Privilege, Social Power, and Inclusion  │  │
│  └───────────────────────────────────────────────────┘  │
```

American Born, Superior White, Heterosexual, Christian, Physically Able, Men

American Born, Pedestalized White, Heterosexual, Christian, Physically Able, Women

American Born, Endangered Black, Heterosexual, Christian, Physically Able, Men

American Born, Strong Black, Heterosexual, Christian, Physically Able, Women

Unearned Burden, Powerlessness, and Exclusion

THE AMERICAN PRIVILEGE PYRAMID SUPPORTS THE CREATION, SUS-
tenance, and distribution of unearned power and privilege in
American society. Unearned privilege is a *culture-based condition* that shapes our thinking, values, beliefs, judgments, loy-
alties, and behaviors toward all members of society and, more
importantly, toward ourselves. As a result, social advantages
like praise, inclusion, forgiveness, trust, opportunity, and power
are fearlessly (we will talk more about F.E.A.R., False Evidence
Appearing Real, in the next chapter) assigned to certain members of a society and denied to others for reasons that have little

if any direct relation to individual effort, character, competency, potential, or tenure.

For example, you may have heard about the interesting statistic that men who are six feet or taller are paid several thousand dollars more per year on average than men who are less than six feet tall. Since a man's height can't be controlled by his effort, character, competency, potential, or tenure, tall men receive a financial and economic benefit for something totally outside of their control or responsibility. They are not formally notified of this unearned benefit in the hiring or promotion process. Often, the person extending the career opportunity and extra height-based salary bias isn't intentionally discriminating against men who are shorter than six feet tall. Rather, they are thinking at that moment, "Wow, what a good fit! This candidate is our kinda guy. Let's do whatever it takes to make him happy because we want him to work for us."

The same unearned height-based privilege statistic does not apply to women who are six feet or taller, and may even represent an unearned burden for some tall women in the workplace. Unearned privilege and unearned burden are handled differently since most people are more willing to acknowledge the ways in which they incur unfair risks (burden) in their lives than unfair advantages (privilege).

The American privilege pyramid affects all communities in the United States. Many immigrant communities comprise people of darker color, and when their new members arrive in the United States to build their lives, they learn all too quickly about the power of skin hue. They are swiftly educated in the myths and stereotypes about people of darker hues and lighter hues. In time, they are assigned their relative position in the pyramid and begin their private battles with the burden of their skin color.

At the top of the pyramid is a private and sometimes unconscious battle with the guilt and fear that accompanies unearned privilege. The beneficiaries of unearned privilege often feel as powerless toward it as those who live near the bottom of the pyramid. They may worry that they will be "discovered" and that those further down the pyramid will threaten their good fortune. Even worse, many secretly fear that the tables of unearned privilege will turn against them. Toward the bottom of the pyramid, people often battle against the rage and self-hate that can haunt you when you live under a system that denies you equal voice, accurate representation, and open access to the qualities of a humane existence. While everyone in a myth- and stereotype-based social power system is a target, for those who are denied social power, the personal consequences are more severe. The truth about their humanity is suppressed, their voices are muffled and replaced with rhetoric, and their true identities are mutilated beyond their own recognition.

I liken this to the world in the movie *The Matrix*. Machines created the matrix to ensure their dominance over mankind, and to use mankind to fuel and sustain the machines' livelihood. The matrix was invisible to everyone except the self-loving and self-aware few whose purpose in life was to live outside of the matrix and destroy it. Through transcending fear with love, self-care, and joy, we too can bring about the destruction of fear-based systems and fear-induced thinking. Only by embracing love of self, and love of mankind, does the whole truth about the world we live in become clear.

Today's myth-infected Strong Black Women stand strong because the American social mythology and power system has convinced them that it is the only way they can ensure their survival. But what about ensuring their right to love and be loved wholly as women and human beings? Placing strength to the side, racism and sexism have prevented us from illustrating the beauty and infinite possibilities of black women, black men, and black love.

The Strong Black Woman Archetype

STRONG BLACK WOMEN ARE NOT BORN, THEY ARE BRED. THEY ARE bred out of an archetype that has been formed from the commingled experiences of gender and race throughout human history. The great psychoanalyst Carl Jung defined an archetype as "an inherited pattern of identity, behavior, emotion, thought, and symbolic imagery derived from past collective experience and passed down to the present in the individual unconscious." Most importantly, archetypes guide how you give and take energy in your all of your love relationships. In essence, being a Strong Black Woman is more implanted than taught. It is something that most black women pick up in childhood from their parental and family history. Realizing the presence of the Strong Black Women archetype in your responses to life (both intentional and unintentional) is the first step to releasing it.

Sometimes we live well into adulthood before we see the power of archetype operating in our lives and the lives of our loved ones. Such was the case for Natalie; few women better typify the range of experiences many professionally successful Strong Black Women have gone through. In the middle of a failing marriage, Natalie realized how much her life choices and circumstances had been influenced by the Strong Black Woman archetype.

"I grew up in a small farming community in the South," Natalie explained. "At age fifteen, my mother, a farm girl herself, married my father, a young, rebellious, streetwise brother from the other side of town. I was the first of nine children and learned very quickly that I had to be strong for my mother and for my brothers and sisters. At the age of five, I was carrying my newborn baby brother on my hip around the house. I never had the time to play with baby dolls like other girls because I was busy helping to care for him like he was my own child. Life was always tough for my mother. My father, a gambling, drinking, womanizing party animal, spent most of his time physically and emotionally abusing my mother. The rest of his time he spent over in the next county at the pool hall with the fellas. We never had enough money for even the basic things. Often, we only had bread and mayonnaise to eat for dinner. Finally, Mom got a job on the graveyard shift at the diner off the interstate. That meant that at night I was left home all alone to care for my brothers and sisters. When Dad was home, he was usually sleeping off his liquor.

"Even with all his evil ways, I still loved my father. I hoped that if I was a good girl and made him proud, he would become the type of father I dreamed of. I heard that one of his pool-hall buddies found the Lord and almost instantly transformed into a loving husband, father, and model citizen. I used to always ask Mom to pray for Dad to find the Lord. She would say that God had no use for Daddy, that Daddy was the 'Devil's soldier.'

"My way out of the life I lived as a little farm girl was to study and make good grades. Markus was the only boy I dated in high school. He was good to me, but didn't care much for my father. Mom liked him, but wasn't too interested in me getting serious about any boy. She wanted more for me than she allowed for herself.

"Markus was a kind and God-fearing brother who had a gift for fixing things. He wasn't the best at his studies, but he always had a car to get around in and a few dollars in his pocket. I knew he loved me, and I thought I loved him, but I was afraid that he would not be able to provide me the financial security that I believed a more educated college man would. It seemed to me that Markus didn't want much out of life except a simple job, a decent car, and to stay in our hometown. I wanted more out of life and out of the men in my life.

"I graduated high school as class valedictorian and left my hometown with a full scholarship to the university a few states over. While in college, I continued to work part-time to help out at home and still managed to maintain a 3.8 average. When I graduated, I wanted a secure job, so I took one with a large bank in New York City and got my MBA in the executive program at a prestigious New York university. I made more money than I thought a black girl could make during those days. Growing up with little to nothing, I had learned how to stretch a dollar. It wasn't long before I owned my first condo and car. All I wanted now was a husband.

"When I turned twenty-seven, I met Carson at a National Black MBA convention. He was an only child from a solidly middle-class New England family. Carson was fine. He was smart, charming, bright as a whip, and a newly minted Ivy League–educated lawyer. My girlfriends saw all that in him, but said he was spoiled and suffered from only-child syndrome. I didn't care because I figured a man like Carson could only go one place in life: up. So I set out to get that man!

"It didn't take long, two years to be exact, before we were

married. By my thirtieth birthday, I was with child, our first son, Jason. I wasn't really interested in having a house full of children, but I did want to give Carson and my parents a man-child. Life seemed to be going according to plan—great job, loving husband, and healthy child.

"Five years passed and it seemed like my life had changed right before my eyes. The problem was that my eyes were shut while all the changes were happening. Carson had worked at three different law firms and was miserable. Life in New York was very expensive, and while both of us made healthy incomes, every penny was needed to maintain our lifestyle. Perhaps that is why I was shocked when Carson came home and announced he had resigned from his fourth job in four years. He had decided to go into private practice and use the den as his home office. Honey, I tried to rip a new butt in him! I mean, we were a team, a partnership and responsible parents to our young child. How could he just make an arbitrary decision to quit his job without any discussion or agreement from me? After weeks of arguing, Carson just shut down on me. We wouldn't talk for days except to answer Jason's questions. It was bad and getting worse.

"This was the beginning of the end, and I should have seen it coming. The private-practice, home-based law firm idea was doomed. Before I knew it, I was bringing home all the bacon, frying it up in the pan, and cleaning the dishes! He just seemed to blame it all on the white man and the system. That gave Carson permission to cry 'poor me!' and drop all the weight of this family on my shoulders. Like a Strong Black Fool, I let him do it. I felt stuck and I didn't know what to do, so for a long time, I just dealt with it. Being a Strong Black Woman means we know how to deal with the shit life throws in front of us. It makes you hard, but you learn to take a lot in stride.

"When Jason entered second grade, I went to a parent-teacher conference and was not prepared for what was about to happen. Jason's teacher gave me a picture Jason had drawn of our family. The picture was Mommy washing dishes at the sink with a sad face, Daddy looking away from Mommy with a sad face, and Jason looking up to the sky with a sad face. My heart sank. I realized he was searching for answers and an understanding of what had become a very tense and unhappy home. Kids are smart. They know what is going on between the sweet words and fake assurances we give to them. It was time to make some changes.

"I filed for a divorce. Carson and I had long since stopped communicating and working at our marriage. We were just going through the motions for Jason. But what I realized that day was that I was also teaching my son how to relate to women through my relationship with his father. Carson had given up his personal power and become even more angry with the world. For two years I polished off my superhero costume and stepped in to save the day. Believe me, this didn't help the situation. The result was disastrous. All of a sudden, I was taking care of two kids instead of one. I finally got it—what my mother must have felt like—but I was not going to live a revamped version of her life. So I got my walkin' papers and I walked.

"After our divorce, I kept Jason and took a job transfer to Washington, D.C. Carson stayed underemployed for several more years and eventually moved back home to his parents' house. As fate would have it, I reconnected with Markus, my high-school sweetheart, who had also been recently divorced. He had never left the area and had opened a few small local businesses.

"Jason and Markus hit it off immediately. And Markus and I have been dating for a year now and are considering marriage. What I learned is that I was more of a factor in why my marriage failed than I could see at the time. My selection of Carson as the perfect man for me was in total accord with my experiences growing up as a Strong Little Black Girl. In the end, I chose Carson so that I could remain that Strong Little Black Girl who took care of everybody and never had time to play with her own dolls. I can see now the ways in which my Strong Black Woman dramas blocked him from stepping up to the plate. I am not taking all the blame in this, but I realize now that being a Strong Black Woman could have kept me unhappy and alone in what appeared to the outside world to be a fairy-tale life.

"Now, I am strong some days and weak on others. I cry when life hurts and ask for help when I need it. And the two men in my life now (my son and Markus) don't need my strength. Instead, they want my love. I finally learned how to allow myself to be with someone who wants to share life's load and be a partner in my happiness. This was something my mother, the Strong Black Woman that she was, never had."

Natalie's experience should remind us that we must engage life on multiple levels. As members of a larger society and culture, we must work vigilantly to dismantle the myths that secure our powerlessness in the social power pyramid of American society. As black men and women, we must compassionately confront the archetypes that get passed down to us from generation to generation. By doing both, we create our best opportunity to free ourselves and the generations that follow from the pain and trauma of our collective history.

AFFIRMATION

Today I don't have to be Wonder Woman,
I just have to take care of myself.
In return, the rest of the world will learn
to take better care of itself.

3 ABANDONED SHIPS:
BLACK WOMEN HEALING FROM LOSS
(ROMANTIC, PLATONIC, SELF-LOVE)

When my father and mother forsake me,
then the Lord will take me up. Psalms 27:10

FOR MANY BLACK WOMEN, BEING STRONG MEANS NEVER LETTING anybody have the chance to do wrong by you ever again. If you live long enough, sooner or later, somebody you love is going to forsake you. They are going to break your heart, let you down, stand you up, kick you to the curb. When this happens you may experience what is commonly called "abandonment." When left unhealed, abandonment can profoundly shape how you participate in relationships for the rest of your life. Susan Anderson, author of *The Journey from Abandonment to Healing,* offers the following examples of abandonment:

- A feeling of isolation within a relationship
- An intense feeling of devastation when a relationship ends
- An aloneness not by choice
- A baby left on the doorstep
- A woman whose husband of twenty years leaves her for another woman
- A man whose fiancée left him for someone more successful
- Children being left by their mother or father
- A friend feeling deserted by a friend

- A child whose pet dies

- A child who feels replaced by the birth of another sibling

- A child feeling restless due to a parent's emotional unavailability

- A boy or girl realizing that he/she is gay or lesbian and anticipating the reaction of parents and friends

- Teenagers feeling that their hearts are actually broken

- A woman whose now-grown children have left home

- People who have lost their jobs and with it their professional identity, financial security, and status

- A dying woman who fears being abandoned by loved ones more than she fears pain and death

Abandonment is all of this and more.

Strong Black Women respond to abandonment in a number of ways, but two stand out for me, particularly in platonic and romantic relationships. They either love harder and more desperately than before, or they build a wall around their heart as thick as the one around Fort Knox. In either scenario, the heart of the Strong Black Women is desperately attempting to either deny or heal from the wounds of abandonment. Worse, neither approach will attract or keep the good lovin' they deserve.

When we are abandoned, several questions tend to run through our minds: What did I do to deserve this? Does this mean that you don't love me anymore? And finally (the question that most often separates the girls from the boys), how can I love you enough so that this won't happen again?

I used to wonder why many women continue to invest their trust in relationships with men who end up taking advantage of them. On several occasions I've become frustrated with female friends who I felt were wasting their time and energy on bozos. I would tell them to "stop trusting men blindly." In a conversation with a dear friend of mine, she pointed out something that I didn't realize. Women don't necessarily trust men blindly, but they do believe in the idea of relationship and partnership. In the face of an unhealthy relationship, many black women ask themselves, how can I keep this dog-and-pony show going? Even if they don't trust their man, they keep on giving because they strongly believe in the idea of relationship. Remember what another friend told me earlier: "The ultimate test of strength for a Strong Black Woman is how to get a man and keep a man." Learning how to make better choices about which men are ready, willing, and able to be in the type of relationship you desire ensures that you won't end up with three dogs, two ponies, and no show. In other words, by choosing to enter relationships with the potential for staying power, you will lessen the likelihood of being abandoned.

For most of us, though, experiencing some form of abandonment is an inevitable part of life. When the circumstances surrounding your abandonment experience cut deep, you can develop a fear of abandonment that you carry into other areas of your life. In your attempt to shield yourself from those who might forsake you, you can unintentionally stop those who truly want to love you from fully participating in your life. How does your strength show up when you *fear* that somebody is going to abandon you? How does that fearfulness color your relationships? What have been some of the personal costs you incurred because of how you handled being abandoned? Have your recurring fears ever set the stage for a repeat performance of past abandonment dramas?

I ran across this cry for help on a relationship message board on the internet: "I push people away. I am in a relationship with a man I really want to be with, and I'm so fearful he will leave that I'm setting him/us up for it to happen. How do I stop? What do I do? Please help me."

Does this sound like anyone you know? When it comes to abandonment, fear can sometimes overpower love. When this happens you have to take the time to understand how the abandonment drama occurring in your life is linked to the lessons about abandonment that you learned during childhood.

Transferring Your Emotional Energy

MOST OF OUR EARLIEST ABANDONMENT EXPERIENCES CREATED "scripts" that were first played out with our mothers, fathers, and other family members. Left unresolved, those scripts begin to play out in our adult lives in the platonic and romantic relationships we form with others. We all play out our scripts on the stage of life until finally we say, "No More Drama!"

In each interaction we have with another human being, there is an emotional exchange. While the circumstances surrounding that energy transfer may just take up a moment in time, the record of that exchange is contained in your psyche forever. Have you ever been on the elevator with a perfect stranger who you sensed as having a bad attitude? That feeling is created because we either pick up on the energy of that person at that moment, or we project the current of our own energy on that person. For example, people who have a positive outlook on life often experience the world and the people who live in it positively. When negative experiences happen in the lives of positive people, they are able to see those experiences as separate events—not as part of an entire web of negativity that surrounds and entraps them, which is the way a negative-minded person might see that kind of experience.

Acknowledging a negative event or a positive event for exactly what it is means something different from denying the significance and impact of that event in your life. Often Strong Black Women respond to negative events with a poker face, while on the inside their feelings are swirling out of control. One Strong Black Woman told me that as a little girl she was warned by her mother, "Don't you cry, because you will chase away your angels!" When you hide or deny the impact of any event in your life, it doesn't go away—rather, think of it as forming a pothole in your emotional highway. Potholes grow bigger with time and wear. The next time events in your life take you back down your emotional highway, you must drive around the potholes, or you'll sink right into them and risk damaging the relationship you are traveling in at that moment.

Remember—it is not enough to "get over it." You must patch those emotional potholes or risk losing control.

Here are the ABCs of emotional energy transfer:

A. We all live in the same world, but the energy we bring to it shapes our individual thoughts, emotions, behaviors, and experiences.

B. We bring the energy and emotions from past experiences into every ongoing moment of our lives and relationships.

C. All of your relationships are sacred spaces. (More about this to come.)

Thus, in many crucial ways, your life is the sum of your relationships. Since relationships are major exchanges of emotional energy, how you manage that energy powerfully affects the quality of your emotional life.

Patching the Emotional Potholes of Abandonment

I'VE HEARD A LOT OF ABANDONMENT STORIES FROM STRONG BLACK Women. Through my listening, I learned that many Strong Black Women have taken the heat or the blame for failed or abandoned relationships. Even more blame themselves. Many of the stories were the "he-done-me-wrong" songs where the "no-good man" and the "good [strong] woman" hook up and create all kinds of drama. She gives him all her good lovin' and he takes it and runs. Meanwhile, she is left alone to pick up the pieces. Drama, drama, drama! That story line has more going on than meets the eye because it is just too simple to be totally true. Please, my sisters and brothers, stop the blame game! Remember, all relationships have a higher goal: to teach us how to love and be loved fully. Good or bad, we can learn and grow just as much from our losses as from our triumphs in life. Blame adds no value to the equation of love.

Take a closer look at why you allow certain people into your life. Remember that stepping into the mythological role of the

Strong Black Woman is like casting yourself in the lead role of an old script that has been passed down to you through generational memory. Ask yourself, what script am I playing in this situation? What supporting roles have I scripted for other people in this situation? Where did I get this script and how many times have I played it before? How does this script support my goal to love and be loved? What would happen if I simply decided to release myself from this script?

Many black women manage their abandonment dramas by shutting down emotions and intimacy. Avoiding emotional drama doesn't mean that you have abandoned old, unhealthy scripts. Rather, it turns the drama inward while reinforcing your emotional detachment from the world. This detachment plays into the social myth of Strong Black Woman as cold and heartless. In this way, strength becomes a form of self-abandonment. You become too strong for your own good.

I also spoke with several churchgoing sisters who live by the "God is the only man I need" script. I ask you to consider a simple question. Is God asking you to deny yourself the experience of a God-fearing partner with whom to share life? Closing yourself off from the possibility of a loving and intimate relationship means missing out on one of the most important parts of your journey to higher love. If God wanted Mary to have Joseph in her life, then why wouldn't he want you to have a loving man in your life, too? Do you believe that your Joseph is out there?

Patching your inner emotional potholes attracts good people into your life. Consider the story of Charlene, a sixty-year-old sister from California. Charlene talked to me about how her unresolved feelings about being abandoned by her mother created a life of bad relationships and bad personal choices.

"I was the daughter that my mother never wanted. She married young and already had another child by her first husband when she met my dad. I don't believe that my mother ever trusted men, so she kept choosing men to marry whom she knew she couldn't trust. There is no doubt in my mind that my dad was not a good husband. He wasn't a good father, for that matter. But my mother seemed to take her anger and hurt out on me instead of my father. My father liked to drink, and he didn't hold his liquor too well. So when he drank, he would emotionally abuse my mother. As a young girl I remember them screaming and fighting. In time the abuse became physical. Thank God my mother had enough strength to leave before she was really hurt. But what came next I didn't plan for. My mother took me to my father's mother and told her that if she didn't take care of me, I would be dropped off at an orphanage. Now I never heard those words come from my mother's mouth, but my paternal grandmother sure didn't miss an opportunity to tell me how my mother was gonna leave me with the nuns.

"I realize that life for a twice-divorced black woman with two young kids in the 1940s was hard. I understand that she was doing what she thought was best, but her resentment toward me was also her way of getting back at my father and his family. I felt like a burden that nobody wanted to assume.

"Over the years I did everything I could to get my mother's approval. I knew that in her own way she loved me, but I wanted her to like me, too. She adored my older half-brother. It seemed she adored everything about him. She would tell me, 'Girls are trouble. They get pregnant, have babies, and dump them off with their mothers.' She often would say, 'You will grow up and try to populate the world because that is what little black girls like you do.'

"You see, my mother was color struck. I took my father's blue-black complexion, while my mother had a pretty brown hue with high Indian cheekbones and a straight nose. My half-brother looked more like my mother, and people were often shocked when they discovered that we were related. I remember when my first daughter was born, Mom came to the hospital to see the baby and said to me, 'Charlene, as soon as you get home you need to start pinching that little baby's nose cause it is spread all across her face.' I said, 'Well, Mom, that's too bad because she is your namesake.' Mom was shocked and pleasantly surprised that I would name my first-born daughter after her. The next day she came back to the hospital and said to the nurse, 'Look at my little namesake, isn't she the cutest little thing you have ever seen?'

I inherited a lot of my mother's unresolved pain. It was hard learning to love myself and even harder finding a man who I believed would love me as I am.

"Well, as I look at my life now, a lot of what my mother said came true. My mother and I spent years arguing and fighting, while I suffered through two unhappy and abusive marriages. I also picked up my father's drinking habit. For many years I could only tell my mother how much she had hurt me after I had one too many Johnnie Walkers. My life has not been easy, but with age I have begun to lay my burdens down. Doing so has helped me to clearly see the course my life has taken.

"About ten years ago, after two no-good husbands, eight children, umpteen grandbabies, and several no-good boyfriends, I met Lloyd. For the first time in my life, I felt a sense of calm when I was with a man. I realized through my relationship with Lloyd that, just like my mother, I had always chosen men who I knew would abandon me. Lloyd was the first man ever in my life who I believed was not going to come into my life, mess around for a while, and then leave. I had grown tired of the other men, and I wasn't even looking for a relationship. Lloyd showed up at a time in my life when I was still. I was calm and content being with myself and by myself. I am glad that I never gave up on relationships like a lot of women I know. That would have made me cold and empty, and I didn't want that. After years of making bad choices with men and everything else, I just didn't know what to do next, so I just became still.

"Now I am beyond the most productive years of my life. I never took advantage of going to school, even though I was as smart as a whip. I have health problems that are a direct consequence of years of abuse to my body, but I am taking better care of myself today than ever before. The kids are grown up and on their own, and finally I have time to focus on myself. I have a good relationship with my kids. I never abandoned them. My mother loves them and they have a decent relationship with her. Mom and I get along much better now that she is older and has changed some of her ways, but it was a long and tough road. We cried and fought and cried some more. But we do love each other and neither one of us is perfect. I forgive her for not being the mother I always wanted. Now we are working on just being friends."

Practice Being Still and Protecting Your Sacred Space

I WAS PARTICULARLY INTRIGUED BY CHARLENE'S COMMENT THAT SHE had been "still" when Lloyd showed up in her life. To be still is one of the most loving things black women can do for themselves. When you are still, you have a better chance of attracting people into your life who will honor your peace, rather than upset it. Being still is one of the best expressions of self-caretaking available to us. When you are still, you are pausing to examine the quality of the emotional energy that is active in your mind, heart, body, and soul. That energy is the same energy you have been reinvesting in your love relationships. Through being still you can begin to appreciate and honor all of your relationships (romantic, platonic, self) as sacred spaces. All loving relationships are sacred spaces. Begin to think of them as a sanctuary and begin to behave in them as if you were in that sanctuary. In other words, think of your loving relationships as a space where you can rest, heal, renew, give, take, grow, and create.

Start by embracing self-care in all of your relationships. By treating others with compassion, you can show them how to be in the right kind of relationship with you. I have heard that many Strong Black Women, after a day of fighting on the battlefield of life, come home to their loved ones still in attack-and-destroy mode. Please, don't kick the dog or whip the cat just because you didn't practice self-care during the day. Furthermore, don't expect the people (or pets) who love you to stand around while you take it out on them. Instead, take some time for yourself. Announce to your loved ones that you need some "me time." Go someplace alone and regroup. Dumping the negative energy of a long, hard day or a souring personal or professional relationship into the unsuspecting lap of a loved one will eventually desecrate everything that is special and sacred about that relationship.

Are you using a friendship or romantic relationship as a dumping ground for things that are negative in your life? Do you like to chronically complain or worry to your loved ones about things that they have little responsibility for or control over? Do you believe that your friends should be willing to put up with your negative attitude or issues, no matter what? If so, you are probably using your loving relationships as a dumping ground. Your loved ones will appreciate you and trust your love for them much more if you have first demonstrated that you are equally committed to appreciating yourself. I am not suggesting that we can't go to our friends, families, and loved ones for support and strength, but I am suggesting that if we bring those challenges into our sacred relationships and do nothing more than gripe and moan about our situations, then we are not honoring sacred space. Your emotionally healthy loved ones want you to do what you need to do to be happy. If they truly love you, they will support the realization of your happiness. It is possible that when Charlene met Lloyd and talked about the calm she experienced with him, she was really experiencing for the first time how to enter into and participate in a romantic relationship without sacrificing the inner peace she had cultivated while she was alone with herself.

Sisterly Abandonment

ALL BLACK WOMEN ARE NOT CREATED THE SAME. THEY DON'T LOOK, think, feel, speak, dress, or love the same. These differences can be the source of a lot of jealousy, pain, disappointment, and even abandonment among black women. Recently, I was on the subway with my friend, Leslie. She is a beautiful, classy, Strong Black Woman with an impeccable sense of style. While we were on the subway, Leslie overheard another sister's boyfriend comment on a ring Leslie was wearing. Without considering the origin of her hostility, the young sister snarled back at her boyfriend, "That ring ain't real!" She then proceeded to bat her eyes and buck her teeth at Leslie as if Leslie had done something to cause her boyfriend to admire the ring. I was so shocked by this young woman's behavior that I burst into laughter. Leslie then turned to me with sadness on her face and said, "Remember this moment for your book. Sometimes my own sisters can be my worst enemies and my greatest disappointment." I paused to consider what happened in that brief moment and the impact it made on Leslie's spirit. (And for the record, Leslie's ring is real!)

Black women and men abandon each other because of competition, jealousy, socioeconomic status, ageism, homophobia, marrying outside of the race, weight and physical appearance, nationality, level of education, complexion, hair texture, dialect, even sorority and fraternity affiliation. Why do we allow these differences to give us permission to cause each other pain? Sisterly abandonment starts when we are kids on the playground and continues throughout life. No matter the age or circumstances, abandonment is driven by the same negative energy.

When outsiders observe members of our tribe abandoning each other, they see it as a curious behavior that illuminates the self-hatred of the abandoner and the fear and sometimes helplessness of the abandoned. Connie, a young, intelligent, silky-haired, caramel-complexioned black woman, shared with me one of the many experiences of sisterly abandonment she has endured.

"I was in ninth grade, my last year of junior high school, and I had already been bullied in the previous years by this girl named Gretchen. Her gang of soul sistas hated me for many reasons: my articulation, my skin color, my hair, and my intelligence; I did seventh and eighth grades in one year and that really pissed them off.

"Early one school day while at my locker, Gretchen bumped into me and whispered in my ear, 'Today, I'm going to cut your face after school. You betta not try and hide because I'll find yo ass. You hear me, bitch?'

"I was mortified. I dropped all the books I had pulled out of my locker and began to cry. Silently, of course, because I didn't want anyone to know that Gretchen had gotten to me.

"I did tell my two best friends in first-hour class, Melissa and Angela, who were hated as much as I was—Melissa for the same reasons as me, but Angela, they just hated because of her dark skin, because she 'talked white,' and because she was a helluva athlete. They tried to convince me to tell my counselor, Mr. Booker.

I said, 'No way, that will just make her angrier and then she'll try to kill me if I get her in trouble!'

"So after each class, Gretchen would walk by me, pull out her switchblade, and pop the blade in and out of the casing, just to reinforce that she was not playin' with me. I was scared shitless. My friends and I tried to figure out a way that I could escape out a back door and run home. Just when we thought we had a plan, one of her goons walked up to us in fifth period and said, 'And don't even think about trying to run outta the back. One us will be at each of the doors to tell Gretchen which one you are coming outta.' My heart sank! All of us started crying on our way to sixth period, the last class of the day.

"With about thirty minutes left in sixth period, my counselor, Mr. Rudy T. Booker, a confident black man of great presence, walked in and told my teacher that he needed to see me. Mr. Booker told me to grab my things and come with him. I looked at my friends in bewilderment, like 'What's going on?' My friends just shrugged their shoulders.

Mr. Booker took me out in the hall and said, 'Connie, I have been informed that you are in serious danger, and I am personally driving you home.' I was overwhelmed and couldn't believe my good fortune. He and I walked out of the front door of the school and got in his car. I saw none of Gretchen and her crew. We rode in silence until he made the right turn onto Lafayette Street where I lived. I quietly said, 'Mr. Booker, how did you find out?' He slowly turned to me and said, 'Vicky Sanchez.'

"Now, Vicky Sanchez was the finest Puerto Rican chick at our school. She kicked ass and took names without asking. She and her crew were also archrivals with Gretchen and her sistas. Vicky lived in the projects of the Black Hills and was proud of it. She and I had talked quietly from time to time when she didn't have to posture for her crew. I thought she kind of liked me, but I didn't trust too many females at that time.

"Vicky found out that Gretchen had threatened me and took matters into her own hands. She and her crew beat Gretchen and her girls to all of the doors of the school, they fought, and then

Vicky told Mr. Booker what had happened. She saved me from being cut.

"I saw Vicky a few days later in the hallway and silently mouthed 'thank you' to her. She, in her cool, face-saving game, gave me a nod of her head to let me know that she recognized my gratitude. She became my quiet friend and protector the rest of the school year.

"I hated that the sistas had to fight, but at the same time, I'm glad I didn't get cut. Most of all, I'm glad that someone noticed that I needed a friend and acted upon making that happen.

"Oh... Gretchen and her crew went to juvie because this was their last chance in the public school system. I never saw them again, ever. I hope we can all become sistas regardless of our race, cultural differences, skin color, hair texture, language, eye color, et cetera. Let's just learn to embrace each other and enjoy being a sista."

We all need to be more willing to acknowledge that Connie's experience is a common one for many young black girls growing up today. Abandonment—sister-to-sister, brother-to-brother, or otherwise—is a result of the lack of social currency allotted to us and accepted by us as a nation within a nation. To fully embrace each other as sisters and brothers, black people must shed social imprinting about our color that divides and conquers us.

Ultimately, abandonment of your brothers and sisters is abandonment of self. I believe that we can step into a larger personhood as black people and ultimately, as human beings. Together we can create a new sense of black identity and community and pride that frees us of our socially contrived patterns of abandonment. To do so we must redefine ourselves as a people who cast off and live outside our heritage of internalized oppression, racism, and sexism.

Are you ready to tear down your stage and rewrite your scripts?

Self-Abandonment

AT THE END OF THE ROAD OF ABANDONMENT IS A DEAD END CALLED self-sabotage. We engage in self-abandonment when we self-sabotage our opportunities to get or give good lovin'. Black women and men continue to experience emotional drama because we choose to place more emphasis in our lives on something *other* than love. Now, I am not saying that just because you choose love, the world will all of a sudden become a beautiful place and strangers will invite you into their homes and fix you homemade cornbread with butter and guava jelly (a personal favorite of mine!). Rather, I am saying that whatever the situation you encounter in life, there is always a loving response or positive course of action that you can take. And when you don't know what that loving course of action is, know that the best recourse is just to be still.

If you are a person of color in the United States of America, you *will* confront abandonment at some point in your life. However, your life is your masterpiece. By stepping off of your abandonment stage and rewriting your scripts, your masterpiece will not only reflect what's excellent and successful about you, it will also acknowledge the role your failures and losses have played in growing your sense of beauty and joy. Self-love is the only weapon you have against self-sabotage.

Often, we sabotage ourselves because of F.E.A.R.—False Evidence Appearing Real. I first heard this acronym several years ago from a participant in a workshop on "radical honesty" given by Brad Blanton. Black women and men who engage in self-sabotage have a lot of F.E.A.R. about love. Much of that F.E.A.R. comes from the mixed messages we see and hear in society today about the nature of true love. We practice self-sabotage because we don't believe enough in our own abilities to recover from the disappointments and betrayals that occur in our lives. We practice self-sabotage because we are afraid to take responsibility for the love we give and the love we want in return.

Loving yourself is a prerequisite to embracing the love you desire from others. But that doesn't meant that getting the love you desire has to be a condition upon which you love yourself. You know the old saying, "Burn me once, shame on you; burn me twice, shame on me." Being burned hurts, and not only makes you angry at the perpetrator, but also with yourself. Sometimes, anger—toward yourself as the victim and toward the entire world as the criminal—is your justification to engage in self-sabotage. But when you engage your world in self-sabotage mode, you are committing a crime against your spirit. In essence, self-sabotage depletes you of your love energy. You have nothing left to give or to take. Think about the state Charlene reached in her life story; finally she arrived at a point she referred to as "tired" and "still." No matter how we get there, we can rebuild from a place of stillness. We can choose a new road that has no dead end, only endless possibilities for a new inner strength called love.

AFFIRMATION

Today my love will overpower any
hurt and abandonment in my life.
I will be gentle with myself.
I will respond victoriously to my fears.
I will embrace my love freely.

4 MAMA AND MINI-ME:
MOTHER/DAUGHTER POWER STRUGGLES
(PLATONIC, SELF-LOVE)

Imagine that we conjure up a world that is safe for mothers and daughters. LOUISE BERNIKOW

MANY TIMES ALONG THE ROAD TO MANHOOD I HEARD THE SAY-ing, "If you want to know what kind of woman your wife is going to be, take a good look at her mother." Curiously, I never heard the same statement made about men; rather, I heard, "If you want to know how your husband will treat you, take a good look at how he treats his mama." In the final analysis, the mother is a trusted measure of a good black woman or man. We are all products of, and in many ways reproductions of, the best and worst of both of our parents.

Mothers in general, and Strong Black Mothers in particular, raise their daughters and sons differently. As author and educator Jawanza Kunjufu once said, "Our mothers love their sons and raise their daughters." Daughters and sons both carve out their core identity by watching and learning from the actions and emotions of their parents while they are growing up. But the Strong Black Woman archetype affects daughters more powerfully because it serves as a model that daughters are expected to follow. Black daughters are imprinted with the positive and negative aspects of their mother's archetype of strength, often in ways they don't understand until later in their lives. Breaking free from this archetype is nearly impossible for some daughters.

However, many of the women I spoke to said while they felt compelled to live up to their mother's Strong Black Woman model when they were young, they were equally compelled to resist much of it as they became more adults. What they were fighting against is not the attribute of strength, but rather to free themselves of the imprints left by our troubled history. American history created the emotional, social, and spiritual burden of mythical strength modeled by Strong Black Women mothers and mother figures, and passed down through them as the appointed carriers of the torch of strength.

The archetype—the myth—of the Strong Black Woman is unique to the black family. It drives all kinds of decisions that shape the character of the black family. Usually, the Strong Black Woman figure in the family, whether the mother, grandmother, big sister, or an aunt, sets the life expectations and rules for all the other members of the family, especially the young girls. They also create models of behavior for young boys. When boys reach manhood, the early influence of the Strong Black Woman myth significantly affects how they behave toward women.

Unfortunately, American history is still a relatively untold and misunderstood legacy of racial, gender, and ethnic brutality. By more closely examining American colonial history, we can gain a deeper appreciation of how the Strong Black Woman myth has functioned as one of the most effective weapons of racial and gender control and oppression. I believe that by better understanding how and why this myth and others like it were created, black people can devise more loving ways to eliminate the toxic problems that continue to contaminate relationships within black families today.

Slavery and the Myth of the Strong Black Woman

IN CHAPTER TWO, I BRIEFLY ADDRESSED THE IMPACT OF SLAVERY ON how black people deal with romantic love. However, much more needs to be said about the impact of slavery on the platonic love shared between black mothers and daughters.

Slavery was built upon the process of breaking the spirits of enslaved African mothers, fathers, and children so they could be dehumanized and controlled by white slave owners as property. Slave owners understood the power of a divide-and-conquer strategy to gain control over the enslaved nation of African Americans. Their goal was to use any means necessary to ensure the cultivation of a wageless labor force. Breaking the spirit of the black slave mother was the key to this system, since both black slave men and women (free labor) were born and nurtured by black slave mothers. Consequently, brutal tactics were used to create a state of trauma-induced independence in the black slave mother.

Trauma-induced independence was the precursor to the myth of *strength* in the lives of black women. In essence, it was the result of the black woman's overtaxed survival instinct. Being strong was the only way for black slave mothers to survive living under the white-supremacist, patriarchal, socioeconomic system that was the slave-holding American South. The survival instinct of black slave mothers created the Strong Black Woman archetype out of their fear for their lives and the lives of their families. In this state of trauma-induced independence, black slave mothers had two choices—be strong or die. Furthermore, they had to be prepared to do whatever was necessary to protect their offspring and loved ones.

American history has reluctantly chronicled the scandalous acts of destruction committed against black slave mothers and their families. For example, in some Southern states, black babies were taken from their mothers and used as alligator bait for white male hunters; male slaves were routinely burned, lynched, decapitated, and castrated in the presence of their wives, mothers, and daughters to reinforce the belief in their minds that they could not depend on black men to be their protectors and providers. Thank God many black women resist believing this about black men today. Many black fathers continue to play a significant and vital role in many black American families. However, too many fathers are still painfully absent from the black American family unit.

Black slave children and husbands were routinely separated from their mothers and wives as they were sold into the plantation system. The goal was to convince the traumatized slave mother that her survival and the survival of her offspring were solely in her hands, because the male slave father would most likely be taken from them at some point. As a result, the oppres-sor could control the slave mother by creating this fear, trauma, and expectation of abandonment. In a trauma-induced effort to ensure the safety of her offspring, many slave mothers attempted to raise their male children to appear to the world as mentally and emotionally weak yet physically strong. This perceived strength and meekness would make them less threatening but still good labor for the slave master.

I experienced a modern-day form of this mothering tactic from my mother. She gave me explicit instructions regarding how to handle myself should I ever be caught alone with a white police officer. She told me, "Toby, you are a big, dark, smart, young black man. The police are going to be scared of you. Any false move, any aggression on your part, will give them justification to shoot first and ask questions later. I don't know what I would do if something happened to you, baby, so, if you ever get pulled over by the police, just be polite, answer their questions, and don't as-sert yourself too much. Do whatever you have to do to get away from them. They would rather see you dead. In the end it would be your word against theirs." Many a day in my lifetime, I have swallowed my outrage and dismay and followed her counsel.

So, for generations, the black woman has been convinced that the black man is not going to be around for long. Consequently, black mothers have raised their black daughters with their own "strength archetype" to ensure their survival in the likely ab-sence of men to protect and provide for them. As a result, many (but not all) black men have had difficulties trying to sustain and honor the family traditions, customs, and practices that char-acterized the balanced African family system prior to slavery. From the perspective of slave owners, destroying family struc-ture and manipulating the black mother's psyche made good business sense.

Today, the legacy of that good business sense is still operat-ing. Black women, and young black women in particular, are more objectified and diminished than any other group of women in the media today. Seventy percent of all black children are born out of wedlock. The prison system houses a nation of black men who have been removed from the pool of available and capable partners for heterosexual black women. Black women are still at the bottom of the economic totem pole, and the black family is for the most part fatherless.

So how does this slave legacy bear upon the relationship between a Strong Black Mother and her daughter today? For starters, it places a heavy burden upon the mother/daughter relationship when the mother must be sole provider and nurturer. The mother must sacrifice much of her own emotional and spiritual sustenance in order to provide for the emotional nurturing of her children. It takes a heavy toll on the mother/daughter relationship when the mother must fight to survive within a sexist and racist society that pounds damaging representations of black life into hearts and minds of girls and boys of all races, creeds, and nationalities. It even takes a toll on the mother/daughter relationship when the support systems of extended family, sisterhood, and community are dismantled because of the internalized oppression, competition, and jealousy that still occur among many black women and men in our community.

It should come as no surprise that most, but not all, of the Strong Black Women I interviewed identified their mothers as Strong Black Women, too. What surprised me was the large number of Strong Black Daughters who commented that while they were thankful for inheriting their mother's strength, it was the "strength myth" that was the root cause of the conflict they encountered in their relationships as adult children of Strong Black Women. They shared many, many examples of how the imprinting they received as children cropped up later in their adult lives to produce self-sabotaging behaviors and to fuel fears that had no basis in either reason or firsthand experience.

These women wanted their mothers to be more human than superhuman, to teach them how to cry when life hurts, when to be weak and when to be strong, and when to ask for help instead of always having to do it on your own. Several of them worry about passing down the strength myth to their own daughters and sons for fear that they will encounter similar conflict later in life. Such was the case for Joanne, a fifty-year-old divorced corporate executive whose mother raised her to be a Strong Black Woman. Joanne's mother later held who she had become against her at a time in her life when Joanne needed her mother the most.

Strength and Betrayal

"MY MOTHER WAS THE SCARLETT O'HARA OF THE BRONX," JOANNE said "She was raised and educated in South Carolina, and grew up with all of the rules that women of her day were taught about men, marriage, and a woman's place in life. I am an only child. My father knew that my mother was a Strong Black Women when he married her. He did a pretty good job of allowing her to be strong, but not letting her get out of control. She would often test the boundaries of their marriage, but they loved each other and that is what kept them together.

"I was raised by my mother and her circle of Strong Black Women friends to be independent and take care of my own business. I guess I took them seriously because I have always tried to live up to their expectations of me. While being strong has been a quality that has helped me to accomplish a lot in my life—a college education, a good job in corporate America, a nice home and car, and all the other trappings—it has created some problems in my personal life. I guess you could say that strength has not been my best advisor when it comes to getting my needs met as a woman. As a matter of fact, being strong has often been a problem for me. For example, when my first marriage was crumbling and I reached out to my mother for help and wisdom, I was betrayed by the very person who imprinted me with her lesson of strength.

"Unbeknown to my mother, I had been suffering silently and desperately in an abusive marriage. My husband, Mr. Nice Guy, was so intent on saving his perfect image that he went to my friends and family and told them that we were splitting up because I was frigid. This was a lie he had devised so he would come out smelling like roses. While I knew his buddies would believe him, I didn't expect the response I got from my mother. When I finally got enough courage to go to my mother and tell her that my husband and I were getting a divorce, I was too late.

He had already gotten to her. Instead of hearing my side of the story, or comforting me, or making sure that I had not been hurt or abused, she blamed me for what was going wrong in my marriage: 'Joanne, if you want to keep your marriage together, then you have to make some changes! I don't care if your husband wants to screw you on the bear rug in front of the fireplace. If that is what he wants, then you need to get down on that floor and screw him.'

"When I heard these words coming out of my mother's mouth, I knew my husband had already spoken to her. What surprised and hurt me most was that she blamed me and told me I was too strong to let my husband be a husband to me. Even as the bright and strong woman that she was, she believed my husband's story without question. Where was her loyalty to me? Where was her motherly intuition? When I would get hurt as a child, she knew that something was wrong even before I could open my mouth to tell her what had happened. But not this time; this time she blindly believed my husband. I was the culprit—the cold, icy wife who was so strong and hard that she wouldn't make love to her husband. These were all lies fabricated by my husband, and even my mother believed them! It was as if everything she gave me to become a good woman, she was now telling me to toss out the window. Even my mother-in-law, another Strong Black Woman, told me that her son left me because I wouldn't let him wear the pants in our marriage. In truth, I was just trying to be strong enough to protect myself from a situation I feared eventually could have killed me. Why couldn't my mother, the Strong Black Woman who raised me to stand up for myself, and take care of myself, and never let anybody walk over me, see what was happening? After that night, I didn't speak to my mother for a very long time. I don't ever recall being angrier with her. For the first time I saw the limits of her Strong Black Woman persona. I also felt betrayed by her for not putting my happiness and safety first. That night she showed her June Cleaver side. When it came to protecting the marriage, even my own safety and well-being were up for grabs.

"Many years later, I told my mother the truth about the abuse I suffered in my marriage. While she was shocked to hear it, she never apologized for not supporting me. What good is being strong if it only means that you are going to be blamed and betrayed when you defend your right to be safe and happy in your relationships? What should I have done instead, sit there and take his abuse for the sake of appearances?

"Virtually every relationship I have had with a man since my husband has in some way reinforced the myth that I am too strong, that I don't need a man. The truth is I have needs, too. I just don't know how to be needy. I want to share my life with someone I can count on, who I know will be there emotionally, spiritually, and in every other way. But if I see that you are jive, I am not going to hang around and take the shit. Life is too short for that! I have a lot of friends who are weak, and they are catching hell just to keep everybody else happy. What bothers me most is that weak or strong, too many of us end up going it alone."

When it comes to being the Strong Black Woman her mother raised her to be, Joanne got more than she bargained for. Should Joanne forget everything her mother taught her about being strong? How much abuse is okay for a woman to tolerate in order to save face with her friends and family? Joanne wanted to be able to express her pain and needs to those she cared about without backlash—in her case, to her mother. Can Strong Black Women like Joanne create relationships with their mothers that allow them to be strong when necessary, yet also vulnerable when they need to be?

Joanne wanted a very different conversation to happen that evening with her mother. She wanted to be heard, not blamed. She wanted compassion and sensitivity, not anger and resentment. She wanted to be held like when she was a little girl and the world became too much for her to bear, but that never happened between this Strong Black Woman and her Strong Black Mother.

Closing the Gap

THE LAST TEN YEARS OF JOANNE'S MOTHER'S LIFE BROUGHT ABOUT a significant shift in their relationship as mother and daughter.

When her mother turned sixty-five, she was diagnosed with Huntington's disease. Joanne assumed sole responsibility for her mother's care. "Realizing that my mother had Huntington's disease answered a lot of questions I had about mother's emotional character. I know that my mother loved me in her own way. While she never told me how proud she was of me, she never stopped beaming to her friends and relatives about my accomplishments. However, when she was diagnosed, it helped me to put the years of emotional chaos that existed in our relationship into perspective. Now, I truly believe that disease is caused in part by our unwillingness to honestly, openly, and effectively handle our emotional lives. Mother was always in conflict within herself because she was trying to meet everybody's expectations of her or forcing her expectations upon others. Learning she had contracted Huntington's disease created a softening in me that allowed more space for compassion toward my mother. Now she only had me to count on, since my father had passed on years before.

"During the ten years I was my mother's sole caregiver, I learned how to love my mother and not let her expectations of me drive my life. I set new boundaries that kept me sane and healthy in our relationship. Even though she was never able to make any real emotional movement toward me, in great part because of her illness, I forgave her. I found a new strength inside myself that allowed me to love her and emotionally protect myself. My mother passed away a few years ago, after a decade of suffering from Huntington's. I miss her and love her."

These kinds of reflections about the often challenging relationships that exist between Strong Black Mothers and Daughters were echoed by many of the women that I interviewed. Yet many Strong Black Mothers and Daughters have successfully created open, honest, and supportive relationships as adults. When I spoke to Strong Black Mothers and Daughters who have good relationships, they identified three key actions that helped them to create, nurture, and sustain respect, honesty, openness, compassion, and love with each other. They are as follows:

1) Listen with a Loving Ear

2) Live and Let Live

3) Develop Compassion Over Blame

They talked about these three actions from both perspectives, mother to daughter and daughter to mother. Here are examples that promote healthy loving relationships in general, and among mothers and daughters in particular.

Listen with a Loving Ear

STRONG BLACK WOMEN WHO HAVE LOVING AND MUTUALLY SUPPORT-ive relationships both as mothers and as daughters talked about the importance of never turning a deaf ear. When we encounter situations that make us uncomfortable, sometimes we simply stop listening. This unhealthy tactic helps us to move back into our comfort zone, but it can damage the bond between a mother and daughter.

Mercedes, a Puerto Rican single mother of two teenage daughters, talked about how she carved out high-quality listening time with her daughters. "My mother never talked about her feelings, much less asked me about what was going on in my life. When my girls were young, I used to read to them at night before they went to bed. They loved the time alone with me, and I realized that spending time alone with their mother before they went to sleep helped them to rest peacefully. The most important part of our bedtime stories wasn't the actual story. Those thirty minutes before bed were also a time for us to talk about how the day went for them and for me, and to pray to God to protect us all through the night. Often my girls would ask me their most intimate questions during this time. Questions like, 'Mommy, why do you love me? Mommy, will you ever marry Papi?' While these questions were tough for me to answer, it helped me to realize the thoughts that were going on inside their little hearts and minds. It also kept a strong and open dialogue going between my girls and me.

"When they became teenagers, story time quickly became replaced with computer chats and never-ending telephone conversations with their girlfriends. I felt like I was losing the openness and sharing we had when they were little girls, at a time when we needed it most. So, each night, about thirty minutes before I would go to bed, I began a new habit called 'pajama talks.' I insisted that once we all were in our pajamas and ready for bed, we would take thirty minutes to talk about the day that had passed and the day before us. This was my time to really listen to my teenage girls. I tried to only ask nonjudgmental questions to see how they felt about topics like drugs, boys, and premarital sex. Rather than lecturing to them, I shared experiences from my teenage years. This was really hard for me to do at first, but I realized it helped them to see me as a whole person, not just their perfect and strong mother. I was trying to be their friend. I know so many mothers who become the enemy, but I didn't want that for my daughters. Thanks to our pajama talks, I have a very open and honest relationship with my daughters. I see their strengths and blind spots. Now I am able to help them find their own way. By listening with a loving ear, I know that they will be able to find their way in life when I can no longer do it for them."

Live and Let Live

NEWS FLASH! A DAUGHTER'S LIFE IS NOT INTENDED TO BE THE LIFE her parents never lived. Rather, it is intended to be the life she is meant to live. Likewise, at some point in the relationship between a Strong Black Mother and her adult offspring, the daughter must expand her perception of her mother beyond her Wonder Woman persona. When this happens, the adult child is first struck by the ways in which her mother's breastplate of strength is tarnished and flawed.

Most mothers (but clearly not all) try to raise their families to the best of their ability. But for every mother there comes a day when her children start acting as if she can't do anything right. What appears to be an act of rebellion is actually her child's attempt to break free from her and her years of caregiving, strength, and guidance. This is all part of the healthy process through which children strive to become self-actualized adults. When this happens, mothers shouldn't relinquish all control and let them run wild, but it also doesn't help to try to overprotect children from the harsh realities and difficult choices that they will have to face in life. Rather, mothers have to help their children understand the cause-and-effect equation that their feelings, thoughts, and actions will have on the love they are trying to get and give in their lives. Doing so requires the right combination of words and actions that will promote openness and honesty.

Marlene, a forty-six-year-old mother of three, talked about the way she and her husband agreed to handle parenting their oldest daughter once she left for college. "My daughter is a talented, confident, and strong young woman. But I was terrified when it was time for her to go to college. I wanted her to become her own woman and live her own life, but the world is so different from when I was her age. It terrifies me to think she is out there having to make all of life's decisions on her own. I know how stupid mistakes can change your life, and I didn't want her to make any of the mistakes that I made as a young woman. I feared those young college boys would take advantage of her and that she might end up pregnant. All the while my husband would remind me that we had done our best, and that the rest was up to her. He would always say, 'Baby, all we can do now is be supportive and allow her to find her own path.'

"During my daughter Cheryl's junior year, she announced she was taking a year off from school to live in Brazil and learn Portuguese. I nearly hit the ceiling and did everything I could to convince her to not to delay her graduation from college. But there was no changing Cheryl's mind. She was moving to Brazil, with or without my blessing. I remember my husband just shaking his head at me. Men don't always understand what it is like to have a child to whom you have devoted your life decide to move halfway around the world.

"After six months, Cheryl invited us to visit her in Salvador de Bahia. When I arrived, I saw my daughter in a way I have never seen her before. She had developed such style and such an open and loving spirit. She seemed totally comfortable and had made many friends who adored her. She was even conversant in the language. I turned to my husband and just from the look in his eye, I knew that we were feeling the same thing—our daughter had become her own woman, a woman who was very different from us in many ways, but who reflected all that we had supported her in becoming and more. Cheryl then came back to the states to finish her senior year, then returned to Brazil and took a job in Rio. She is now living and working in Brazil and embracing a life that I never could have imagined for her. As hard as it was to let go of my daughter, it was worth the effort to see her blossom into her own phenomenal woman."

Develop Compassion Over Blame

COMPASSION BREEDS HONESTY AND FORGIVENESS WHILE BLAME ONLY creates emotional distance, resentment, and guilt. Mothers and daughters who are not getting or giving the love they want and deserve in their relationships with each other can usually point to numerous examples of fault-finding and finger-pointing. Blaming phrases like, "I can't believe you are dragging this up again," "Once and for all, can we please drop this," "How many times do I have to tell you," and "If you really loved me you would," create huge wounds in a relationship that must be healed. Fault-finding is a guaranteed way to destroy the intimacy between a mother and daughter, particularly when they are both Strong Black Women.

Are you the kind of person who is known to have a sharp tongue? Having the last word in arguments only means that the next time you want to have a dialogue with your parent or child, they will not feel safe to participate openly and honestly in the conversation. Even if you call all the shots in the relationship, there is still value in hearing, acknowledging, and respecting both sides of any story. This is one of the ways we nurture the sacred space that is a part of every relationship we share with a loved one. Blame is one of the many ways we can desecrate that sacred space; compassion is one of the best ways to expand it.

Sometimes parents use blame and criticism as a way to maintain control over their children. This can seem like a good choice when they are dealing with a child who is rebellious but doesn't possess the life experience and wisdom to make smart choices. Likewise, children blame their parents as a way of exerting independence and control over their own lives. This is not unique to Strong Black Mothers or Daughters, but rather a universal part of the human condition and something that we all should do a better job of managing in our relationships. When dealing out blame and criticism, we risk creating emotional scars that may take years to heal.

Seeing Clearly by Managing Emotions

MARY, A FORTY-ONE-YEAR-OLD SINGLE MOTHER OF TWO TEENAGE daughters who lives in Miami, learned an important lesson about using compassion instead of fault-finding in her relationship with her eighteen-year-old daughter. Mary realized she had to call upon something other than a blaming attitude and a sharp tongue to convince her "all-grown-up" daughter to resist being negatively influenced by her "bling-bling" girlfriends.

"My daughter came home one day last spring and told me that she and a few of her girlfriends had decided to go to work as exotic dancers at a local strip club in Miami. She said that she knew that I wouldn't like it, but she didn't want me to hear it from anyone else. Let me tell you, when she told me what she was going to do, it was like someone took a brick and hit me in the head. At first I was just shocked; then all of a sudden I became full of anger. I couldn't even look at that willful child, because I felt like she was throwing away all of the sacrifices I had made for her for the past eighteen years. I knew she could tell by my silence, and by the fact that I had to look away from her just to stop myself from slapping the stupid out of her, that I was not going to take this decision without giving her a piece of my mind. But I was so mad, so hurt, and so disappointed in her that all I could do was get up from the kitchen table and go to my bedroom.

"Now, I have never been one who was short on words where raising my daughters was concerned. I had them young, and their father...well, let's just say that he chose crack cocaine over me, so I chose Christ the King over him. I raised my girls without welfare, without handouts, without any man running up in my house just so I could get my rent paid on time. I kept a job, went to school at night and got my GED, and kept a clean and God-fearing home in the projects. I want my girls to have a different life than I have had. Many of my old girlfriends gave up on life long ago. I made my mistakes when I was young, and I have tried all I know how to protect my girls from making the kind of silly mistakes that can ruin your life. I managed to get my oldest through high school without her getting pregnant, and it wasn't easy because she has a strong will like me. We have been going at it since she was thirteen. Her decision to work at a strip club pulled the rug right out from under my feet. You know, some-times you can feel like your kids are out to get you, like they are the enemy. Seems like I have always had to fight an enemy in my life, but never my own flesh and blood.

"Later that day, I called my pastor and told him what had happened. I told him that my daughter had just turned eighteen and I knew that I had no legal power over her. I told him I had decided to tell her to get out of my house, but I knew deep down inside that if I kicked her out of the house, she would be at the mercy of the nightlife and I could lose her forever. But how could I stand by and watch my first born shake her ass all night just so she could keep up with her bling-bling girlfriends who want to make some fast money?

"My pastor listened as I let all my feelings out, and then he said, 'Sometimes when people you love make decisions that you don't like, all you can do is show them how much you love them.' He suggested I sit down with my daughter and rather than tell her why I thought she was making a mistake, I should try to get a better understanding of why she felt a need to dance at a strip club. He pointed out that while my daughter is as strong and willful as I was when I was her age, and still am today, we clash as mother and daughter because we spend more time blaming each other than truly understanding each other. He was right. I have always wanted the best for my girls, but being a single mother has been hard. My girls are all I have, and their success and happiness is all I have to show for my life. He asked me if I had told my daughter some of the things I had told him during our conversation, if I had shared what they really mean in my life. I realized that I hadn't. So pastor suggested that I start the conversation by letting my daughter know what she means to me, rather than doing what I tend to do—letting her know what I expect from her.

"The next day, I went to my daughter and told her that I wanted to talk about what she had told me. I asked her to explain to me why she wanted to work for a strip club and what she hoped to gain from doing that. She told me she wanted to be able to be her own person, have her own money, and to even be able to help out around the house. She also told me that it was the only way she knew of being able to afford the cost of paying for community college. She said it had very little to do with her girlfriends, but that she could make a lot of money.

"I asked my daughter to think about how much money she really needed to make in order to have her own money, pay tuition, and help out around the house. She said she didn't know. I told her that while she was a grown woman, and I had to respect her decision, that I loved her and wanted more for her than to have to work at a strip club. I asked her if she would consider a job as an office assistant since I had a friend who worked in human resources for one of the large express-mail companies. She didn't think she could qualify for a position like that, but I said let's try. Well, God was with us because she was hired on the spot and began work a few weeks later. She loves her job and her co-workers and she has decided to use the employee tuition reimbursement program offered by her company to go to college.

"I learned an important lesson from this experience. I learned that my daughter's real intention in wanting to be an exotic dancer was very different from what I assumed. I learned that my years of finger-pointing and arguing weren't helping me to see the woman that my daughter was struggling to become. My emotions became my blind spot and could have pushed her further away from me. I also learned that when I allow myself to move beyond my fear and anger, I don't need to place blame. Instead I can strive to see, appreciate, and respect the other side of the situation."

By embracing honesty and managing her emotions, both Mary and her daughter were able to behave in a wiser and more loving way. Since this incident, Mary has begun to communicate differently with her younger daughter, too. "I am being more open and honest with both of my girls, especially my younger daughter. I talk about the mistakes I made in my life and the lessons I have learned. This has become the wisdom I share in my relationship with my daughters. I know they have to do their own thing, but at least they will have the benefit of my hard knocks. One more thing—this experience created more trust between me and my eighteen-year-old. She has a good head on her shoulders. I guess I wasn't able to see that until now."

Tips for Improving Mother/Daughter Communication

WHAT FOLLOWS IS A LIST OF SUGGESTIONS I COMPILED FROM THE women I interviewed for this book, all of which are ways to promote healthier mother/daughter relationships. They are intended to encourage openness, honesty, and self-caretaking. Over the next month, try to incorporate these suggestions into your relationships with your parent or children. Each time you find yourself in a situation where you are able to apply one of these suggestions, record the situation and outcome in a diary. After a few months, review the diary to identify any shifts in how you feel and behave, or to note any change in your relationships.

- **Get off the phone gently when a conversation becomes too tense** Agree that it is important to resolve the issue and that you would like to set a time in the near future when you can both revisit the conversation in a calmer manner.

- **Agree to disagree** Sometimes in life we have opposing perspectives and opinions about a situation. When this happens, we may simply have to agree to try to better understand all sides of the issue, and focus on what (if any) aspects of the issue we can try to resolve or improve together. Doing so requires that we take responsibility for the things we have control over as well as recognize those that we can't control. It also means that we have to agree to act in a manner that serves the best interests of everyone, rather than just ourselves.

- **Always close with "I love you"** Make a pact with your parents and children: with no exceptions, no matter if you are happy or mad, end every conversation with your mother or daughter by saying, "I love you." By honoring this pact, you demonstrate the importance of love in dealing with any difficult challenge that life may present to you.

- **Stop digging up the past** Continually rehashing the past almost always creates tension, guilt, and anger in relationships. Instead, take note of the patterns and repeating behaviors that occur in your relationship and work together to prevent them from happening again in the future.

- **Express gratitude freely and frequently** Even mothers and daughters never grow tired of hearing that they are appreciated by each other. When you take the time to let someone know that you appreciate their intentions and their actions, it reinforces the likelihood that they will behave similarly in the future. It also lets them know that you are tuned into their thoughts and feelings, and paying attention to their efforts.

- **Honor all requests for space and time** Have you ever been accused of nagging? Nagging almost always creates avoidance and distance in relationships. Instead of nagging, respect the personal space the other person needs in the relationship (the same kind of space we want for ourselves). This almost always fosters a better relationship. In order to do this, talk about any deadlines that are out of your control and that may have an impact on the situation you're trying to address; also, agree on another time to revisit the situation, so it doesn't slip from anyone's attention.

AFFIRMATION

Today I will make a special effort to love, honor, and protect the sacred space shared between mother and daughter.

5 WHAT MEN WANT FROM AND FOR STRONG BLACK WOMEN (PLATONIC AND ROMANTIC)

THIS CHAPTER IS THE RESULT OF CONVERSATIONS I'VE HAD WITH men who have had romantic and/or platonic relationships with Strong Black Women. These women are their mothers, wives, bosses, sisters, best friends, daughters, mentors, and neighbors. Countless articles have been written about what men want *from* women. However, it seems men are seldom asked how their experiences with Strong Black Women have shaped the hopes, fears and desires they have *for* black women. As a man, I have noticed that a fairly narrow and repetitive set of questions gets raised in cross-gender dialogue. Rather than asking the same old questions, in preparing this book I wanted to spend some time listening more carefully to men as they shared their uncensored relationship experiences.

While their experiences are different, some common themes emerged about sharing life with a Strong Black Woman. Most importantly, the men I interviewed say they see through the armor of strength that takes shape in the lives of many black women. Furthermore, they are aware of the unique struggle that being strong creates in the lives of the black women they know and love. They also agree there is no magic equation to guarantee success in any male/female relationship. Rather, each relationship is as unique as the two people participating in it.

The twenty-five men I spoke with said they often get into big trouble when they try to apply an "all women are this or that" philosophy to figuring out the black women in their lives. As one brother said, "I have met a lot of Strong Black Women in my life and of course they have a lot in common, but there is something about each of them that makes them unique. I can't stereotype all Strong Black Women as high-maintenance or overly aggressive or even God-fearing women. I can't do this because a black woman's strength comes in many different forms and functions. When I figure out what it is about a particular black woman that makes her strong, it makes her weaknesses more apparent. As a good brother, I try to honor a black woman's strength by not playing on her weaknesses. Likewise, a good woman is going to do the same for me. In my opinion, that is what separates a good brother like myself from a dog."

Read carefully the experiences of James, Darryl, Michael, Lenny, Terrell, and Jimmy. I selected their stories to share with you because they represent a broad range of the sentiments that don't get heard or discussed enough in conversations where women are present.

Daddy's Little Girl

JAMES IS A FIFTY-FIVE-YEAR-OLD AFRICAN AMERICAN ENGINEER for a major federal government contactor in the Washington, D.C. area. He and his wife, who have been married for thirty years, have two grown daughters who are in their twenties. Like most fathers, James adores his girls: "I have always wanted the very best for my daughters. Donna, my oldest daughter, is engaged to be married next summer. For the first time, I have had to seriously consider what I want for her as she makes one of the biggest commitments of her life. I consider Donna to be a Strong Black Woman because that is what her mother and I raised her to be. I learned early on that women learn how a man should treat them from observing how their father treats their mother. So my wife and I agreed a long time ago while the girls were still young to do and say whatever was necessary to keep our relationship healthy. We felt it was the only way to help our girls make healthy choices about men later in life.

"Donna graduated in the top 10 percent of her college class and now has a great job in corporate America. She is marrying a man she has known since her freshman year in college. They've been dating for two years. For the most part, Donna has made good choices in the men she's dated. I told her that if she wanted to know if she was dating a good man, then she should bring him home. I would be able to tell after a few interactions if the guy she was dating had her best interest at heart. I am glad I made that offer to Donna, because she never felt like she couldn't bring her romantic interests home to meet the family. I believe that keeping a healthy and nonjudgmental attitude about my daughter's choices in men helped her to make responsible choices and, more importantly, to protect herself. She once told me that she always knew that if a guy could handle himself when he came to meet her parents, then he was probably worth her time and interest. I believe that parents should stay involved in their children's lives, but that doesn't mean we have a right to interfere with their task of finding a spouse. Rather, my role as her father is to listen and make sure she knows what she wants and what she doesn't want from any man in her life. My job as her father is to make sure she knows how to carry herself in such a way that men won't disrespect her or take her lightly.

Furthermore, my job as her father is to let her know she is loved and lovable with or without a man. So many young women today place their self-worth in the praise or attention of men. That is a mistake! I tried to raise my daughters to be whole and emotionally self-sufficient. I reminded them early and often that there is a difference between wanting a relationship and needing a relationship. I also told them that there is a difference between falling in love and being in love.

"I remember Donna came home from high school once with a necklace her boyfriend gave her. It was one of those circles that had been cut in half; she wore one half and he wore the other to symbolize they were two parts of a whole. She was furious when I told her not to wear the necklace because she was 'whole, not half.' She didn't understand what I was getting at then, but she has often referred to it as a moment in our relationship where

I taught her an invaluable lesson—*never lose yourself in a relationship*. That is the essence of what I want for my daughters. I want them to be their own women, independent of the approval or acceptance of any man. I want my daughters to love themselves enough to protect themselves when careers, marriages, or friendships go wrong in life. That can be hard to do if you feel that you are defined by a job, a spouse, or a social circle. I have seen a lot of women sacrifice their self-esteem just to be popular. Popularity ain't love! I tell my daughters that in order to be loved as you are, you must first know who you are, then you must love who you are.

"I am proud of my daughter and I believe she has made a good choice in a fiancé. Marriage is a long and winding road, and you need to have a handle on who you are before you begin the journey. As far as what I want *from* my daughters, this is simple. I want them to always respect their mother and me. I want them to include us in their lives as they move forward. Of course I want grandkids and family outings and all the stuff that will make the later years of my life rich and full. But more than anything else, I want them to defend their right to be happy unconditionally."

Parting Ways

DARRYL, A TWENTY-SEVEN-YEAR-OLD SINGLE PARENT AND POLICE officer from the Midwest, recently ended a five-year relationship with a Strong Black Woman. Darryl's story was similar to those of several of the single men I spoke to who felt that when a woman's strength is combined with her insecurities, it can be a destructive force in an intimate relationship.

"What do I want from a Strong Black Woman? Now that is an interesting question. As a black man, and a strong one at that, I am defined through my experiences with black women. Growing up in the 'hood, my reputation as a man was defined by what the sisters said about me and how they treated me in the presence of other black men and women. So my boys and I spent a lot of time creating and defending our manhood through the fabricated or real experiences we had with women. For example, I lost my virginity when I was sixteen, but I told my girlfriend at the time that I had been sleeping with women since I was thirteen years old. I did it so she would think I was all that!

"Lying is a big part of how a man's identity gets formed in relationship to women. As men, and as black men in particular, we are expected to have certain feelings or not have certain feelings. I don't care what they say in *Essence* magazine, black men don't really get points for being too 'nice' or too much of a 'good guy.' A lot of sisters, even though they won't admit it, really like a hard man. They like the image of us as macho and if we show them anything else, they think we are weak or even gay. It takes a good while before a woman I am dating gets to know the real me. You see, every time you are with a woman, your reputation as a man is being put to the test. We have a lot of pressure to perform as a sister expects.

"Women talk; I have learned that anytime I interact with a sister, my masculinity is being broadcast to the world. When black men and women relate to each other more from their un-challenged assumptions of each other instead of taking the time to get to the truth, it can make it difficult for a brother and a sister to trust each other. That was my number-one issue with the woman I dated for five years. What I have learned as I have grown older and more experienced is how to get clear on what my real needs are and how they may be different from what is culturally and socially expected of me as a black man.

"In order for me to trust a sister enough to share my real needs, I have to know that she is not going to kick me when I am down. That was another huge problem in the relationship I recently ended. She was a wonderful black woman but I never knew when she would turn on me. I need to know where my woman stands emotionally. Excuses like PMS or a bad day at the office just don't hold their weight after a while. I can't commit to a relationship where at any time without notice I can be treated like the enemy. Her emotional roller coaster was so wild that I could never trust her to have my best interests at heart.

"It also seems to me that many Strong Black Women like to be right *all* of the time! Being right was more important to her than protecting our relationship. For the record, I think I am a good catch. I have a lot to offer, but I am not open to some of the battles that happened in my past relationship. It drives me crazy when a woman I am dating forces her insecurities onto the relationship for no valid reason. It means I can never get comfortable with her.

"My last girlfriend was truly a wonderful Strong Black Woman. She was beautiful, smart, college-educated, and a very sweet woman most of the time. But she had an underbelly to her that I could never understand, and that ultimately made it difficult for me to trust her. I felt like she would do me in if she felt I had done her wrong. I realize all woman are different, but I do think that Strong Black Woman oftentimes possess this angry edge that can make it difficult for men to open up to them in relationships. It's like they are always on guard and ready to pounce. Does every sister feel like she has to be on guard, even with the man she loves? Your relationship should not be your battleground. If she had just gotten past this point, we might have had a chance for a future together.

"I keep hearing Strong Black Women complain that all men are dogs, and that's why they have to be on guard in their relationships with men. If you go into a relationship believing that your man is a dog or will become a dog, then how do you learn to treat him as anything other than a dog?

"So what do I want from a Strong Black Woman today and as I move forward? I want a woman who is emotionally responsible and secure. That means she can express her own feelings and emotions in a manner that doesn't always result in doing battle with her man. I want a Strong Black Woman who knows how to release the stress of being black and female, so when she's around me, we can just focus on what we're trying to do and be there for each other. I want a Strong Black Woman who has clearly defined borders and boundaries. Don't say one thing to me, and mean another! That drives me crazy! Most brothers just don't feel safe when a sister plays Jedi mind tricks with them.

"I also want a Strong Black Woman who knows how to keep what goes on between us private. I don't need to hear about our business from her mother or sister or girlfriends. That's a real turnoff. I want a Strong Black Woman who is not afraid to come to me when she has had a tough day and just talk. We all have things that happen in life to make us angry or frustrated, and you should be able to share those things with your man. But remember who the enemy is, and don't let it pollute the time we spend together. Don't make me the enemy, because if you treat me like the enemy, I will begin to act like the enemy.

"As far as what I want for a Strong Black Woman, I am still putting that together in my mind. I'm going to turn thirty soon and I'm ready to settle down and raise my family. I want to be a good husband for a Strong Black Woman. I have dated women from all different cultural backgrounds—Latin, Asian, and white as well as black. Sisters are the only women who I believe in the long run will have your back. If you can find the right Strong Black Woman, one who doesn't carry around a lot of anger and suspicion with her, then you can be sure that you will have a wife who will be *on your side* and *at your side*. In my experience only a Strong Black Woman will be *on your side* and *at your side* when the going gets tough. I don't mean to sound prejudiced, but that is what I have learned from the experiences I have had dating women of different races. There is so much of the black experience in America that just can't be explained unless it is happening to you. Strong Black Women understand that experience because it is the experience that we share as a race of people in America. I don't have to explain or defend myself as a black man in America to a Strong Black Woman because she is catching hell too. In that way she is *on my side,* because she is naturally sensitive to my struggle. It is our struggle to share and overcome together.

"I have big plans for my life, and as a successful black man, people will be out to take pop shots at me. Just look at what happens to our athletes and rap artists. One false move and we get kicked, stomped, and left for dead. I know the world wonders what is wrong with Whitney Houston and Bobby Brown. I know they have a lot of problems, but Whitney is sticking with her man, even if others think he ain't no good! I am not saying that is the right thing for her to do. However, I must admit that as a black man, I want someone who will be with me for better or worse. Having said that, I want to be the kind of man that a Strong Black Woman would be proud to have *at her side.*"

Too Strong for Her Own Good

MICHAEL IS A FORTY-THREE-YEAR-OLD, TWICE-DIVORCED, CORPO-rate executive from the Midwest. His first marriage, which happened when he was in his early twenties, lasted for a year and a half. His second marriage, to a Strong Black Woman, lasted for eleven years and ended in 2000. He has a lot to say about what he wants from and for Strong Black Women.

"First off, let me say that any relationship with a Strong Black Woman, romantic or platonic, is definitely a two-way street. In a relationship where two people have very strong wills, you must have a tough skin, because there are things that need to be communicated even if they aren't complimentary. The primary problem in my last marriage was a lack of open, honest, and timely communication. When you don't say what is really bothering you for fear of hurting the other person, it will eventually come out in other ways like a bad attitude, withdrawal, silence, or even infidelity. I think two strong-willed people have to learn how to communicate even when they're not getting their way with each other. Strong Black Women have strong wills, which can challenge their husband's masculinity in a manner that shuts down effective communication. When this begins to happen in a relationship, the risk to the marriage is significantly increased.

"I was not the perfect husband, but I am a good man. My ex-wife is a wonderful woman, but she was by no means perfect either. I think we overlooked or underestimated one vital element in picking a mate: the establishment and honoring of a shared set of values and goals in life. My wife and I said we wanted the same things out of life, but I realize now that was only on the surface. When the time came to make the tough sacrifices that supported what we both said we wanted, we embraced opposing courses of action. This created big problems, because I firmly believe that marriage is a corporation. A corporation can only have one CEO, and I was raised to believe that the husband is the CEO. At the end of the day, the man has final say on certain decisions that must be made in the best interests of the family. But it doesn't mean that I don't value my wife's input and support. What I have experienced and seen in other marriages is that some Strong Black Women say if you are not gonna give me what I want, then I will go get it anyway. This is one of the reasons that some black men see some black women as too independent. Also, as a husband, I don't like having all of my decisions questioned.

"As a Strong Black Woman, my wife would go off and do what she wanted to do after I thought we had decided to do something else. For example, we both agreed to work hard to create a comfortable and financially stable future. When we started looking to buy a home, we had very different opinions about how much to spend. I wanted to spend in the low $100,000 range and she wanted to spend more than $200,000. I wanted us to grow into a big house so that we would not have to struggle to make the mortgage payments. She didn't want to buy a 'cheap' house. It seemed in the end that we only agreed on one thing, that we both wanted out of the apartment that we had been renting. We never seemed to be able to reach consensus about many things in our marriage. You learn the most about the person you're sharing your life with when the chips are down or they're not getting their way. It's how she handles herself during the tough times that reveals what kind of woman you are involved with.

"We had two cars. Both cars were paid for, and I was between jobs. My wife worked with young kids and decided that she needed a van. I implored her to wait until I was gainfully employed again before taking on another car note, but I might as well have been talking to a wall. She rode me and rode me and rode me until finally I agreed to get an SUV instead of a van. So I plunked down several thousand dollars to buy an SUV. When the car note started coming in and we were struggling, she attacked me and said, 'You need to go out and get a job.' Now if she had waited until I had found another job, this wouldn't have been a problem. Things got so bad that she finally left me while I was unemployed and with a car note that I never wanted in the first place.

"Now, after two marriages, I don't believe in 50-50. No relationship is 50-50. It is the biggest myth when it comes to marriage. Strong Black Women can still be strong while also understanding that sometimes you have to accept things that you are not in support of—and allow them to happen. I had a friend whose wife decided to make a $2,500 dollar investment in Avon products and sales supplies. He knew it was a big mistake because his wife did not have a salesperson personality. He made the investment and as he'd predicted, it was a waste of her time and his money. But he didn't go back to her and say I told you so.

"I also want Strong Black Women to be consistent. Be a good girl or be a bad girl, but don't flip the script. Black women today are in a confused state in terms of their identity. I see more sisters dating married men because it is easy and they don't have to make a commitment. On the dating scene, I think it's OK for a woman to say, 'Hey, I am just in it for the sex,' but don't say one thing and mean another. When I see inconsistency in a Strong Black Woman, I move on.

"What I want for Strong Black Women is for them to learn to separate their feelings from their fears. All black men are not scum of the earth. All black men are not just trying to get some for the evening. black women should learn how to read the signs! Men are tired of being stereotyped. The 'playa playa' type of black man is not the majority. Don't be afraid to share everything. I have learned that you can't have a successful relationship where you are guarded and secretive. Stop doing crazy stuff your mama taught you to do, like keeping mad money. Instead, let's get it all out on the table. The only way to deal with our issues is to resolve them, not keep a stash and scheme for a way to escape from them.

"Strong Black Women are quick to judge men by what we have or don't have. Two can play at this game. I wish Strong Black Women would learn to accept men just the way we are. After being twice divorced, I don't have a lot of patience for this nonsense.

"Don't use sex as a weapon. The rollover in the middle of the night is sure to keep your bed cold and eventually empty. While that is no excuse for a man to go out and have sex with somebody else, it creates a big problem for a man in a committed relationship. Strong Black Women tend to become complacent once their man commits. If you like sex then do what you do, but don't make it a reward and penalty system. Why is it when a woman starts dating she likes it every night? Then, after you marry her, you're lucky if you get it once a month?

"For the record, I want to dispel one of the greatest lies Strong Black Women hold against black men—that we date white women to gain a trophy. For most of the brothers I know, deciding to date a white woman is not about the trophy, it's about being happy. I don't have time to come home to the ongoing battles waged by many Strong Black Women toward their men. Brothers are now saying, I can go in another direction and not have to deal with all the headaches. But black women see it as a trophy thing. They refuse to see their role in why black men date outside of the race.

"I've decided that I'm not gonna wait around for the perfect Strong Black Woman. I'd love to work with you, but at the same time I deserve to be happy. Color isn't a guarantee of love. It also isn't an issue when you meet the right person. I realize it can become a problem when the family gets involved, but between the man and the woman, love is color-blind.

"I've known a lot of Strong Black Women who are simply angry at life. They blame everybody! Everybody owes them for the sins committed against their ancestors. Well, I don't owe Strong Black Women anything. We all start out with a clean slate. If you are so angry that you can't honor the right to happiness in others, then God be with you. At this point in my life, if I can't be happy with you, for sure I can be happier alone."

My Best Friend and Trusted Partner

LENNY IS A FIFTY-YEAR-OLD WHITE FATHER OF TWO WHO HAS BEEN married for fifteen years to a Strong Black Woman. He now works in the nonprofit sector and his wife is a corporate executive.

"Growing up on the periphery of Hollywood, I do not remember there being very many black women. Black people still stand out in Hollywood today. I grew up in an affluent neighborhood in Southern California (the one black student at our high school of

2,250 students was the exchange student from Ethiopia!), so college was the first time I had any interactions with black people.

"I grew up with very liberal, progressive parents who stressed the importance of a good education among other core values. While my mother didn't work when I was growing up, she did go back to the workplace. Consequently, it was very important for me that anyone I married be able to support herself. It was both reflective of what I wanted for her (to be able to take care of herself) and that I didn't want to be the sole provider. I wanted to marry a woman who wanted to be a part of a team. I wanted to marry someone who could be provider and nurturer and would allow me to be the same. I wanted a peer, a partner, and someone I could respect in all ways, not necessarily for the traditional traits, either. Illustrative of that point is the fact that my wife doesn't know how to cook. I tend to do the cooking because she's not very comfortable in the kitchen—in truth, she has very few instincts for cooking at all. That was a surprising discovery, particularly after I learned what a good cook her mother was. But we didn't need two cooks. On the other hand, she has a lot more patience than I do and more nimble fingers, hence, she has generally been the all-purpose assembler in our house. It didn't matter a whit what the traditional roles were supposed to be for us. Both of us were comfortable with the other doing what he or she was better at, though both of us have ventured over the years into the other's areas of skill, developing some useful redundancies. Perhaps it was easier for us to do this than other, single-race couples, because by our very relationship we had left the traditional behind.

"My wife and her sister are both Strong Black Women. My sister-in-law is more willing and likely to display her emotions than my wife. Nonetheless, they are both strong. My wife is more even-tempered and patient. I am more outspoken and volatile, with a shorter temper than my wife. People are sometimes surprised to hear her speak passionately about her convictions because she doesn't hit you over the head with them, rather she more typically acts on them.

"We started dating when we were both in our mid-thirties. When you are dating at that age you move past the small talk pretty early in the process and the tough questions tend to come up quickly. My wife was raised to take care of herself and not look to a man to take care of her. She comes from a family of high achievers who value educational excellence. Her family tree is chock-full of relatives who have graduated at or near the top of their classes and have risen to the top of their professions. Once I met my mother-in-law, I clearly understood how my wife came to be who she is. I adored my mother-in-law. She was a Strong Black Woman who emanated inner beauty, grace, and quiet strength. My mother-in-law was quick, and while she never said anything nasty about anyone, she sure loved it when I did! She was an extremely understanding person. She couldn't do enough for you, and she and I would laugh continuously when we were together. She was very accomplished in her own right (high school valedictorian, integrated a major state university, graduated with a degree in microbiology), yet quiet about her own skills, capabilities, and successes. Through my relationship with my mother-in-law I learned that they embraced the same values as my family. My family recognized my wife's rare qualities and strength from the start and was—rather uncomfortably for us—eager for us to marry well before we were. This has helped us grow as a couple and as a larger connected family from different cultural and racial backgrounds.

"The Strong Black Woman means so many things in society today. For me, it conjures up a broad spectrum of images from the abandoned woman having to raise kids on her own, to the black woman who has worked her way into the corporate world and moves up the ladder. Because of subtle racial prejudices, black women often have to walk in two very different worlds. They have to be a small minority in a white corporate landscape and at the end of the day they become the gender majority in a predominantly black community. I can only imagine how taxing that must be on the black woman's psyche and emotional constitution.

"I want Strong Black Women to take care of their physical and emotional health. Over the years, I've come to realize the emotional and physical toll that many minorities encounter as a consequence of daily life. This has a particular impact on black women, reinforcing many of the myths and stereotypes that exist about them. I've worked with very talented Strong Black Women who, unfortunately, were also extremely obnoxious and offensive. One colleague in the entertainment industry consistently used racism and sexism as excuses to be nasty, selfish, and mean. She was an angry person. When you're filled with negative energy, that is what you attract. It affects your hearing—she could not hear the truth about her work because she labeled everything as racism or sexism. She believed that I couldn't embrace her or her work because I was white. So no matter what, I couldn't win with her. The fact is that some people don't attract honest interactions from others...and that is not a good thing. The entertainment industry is a very challenging business that attracts difficult people for whom less of a toll is taken by offensive behaviors. By necessity, they have tougher skins than other people. But having a tough skin doesn't mean you have to be distasteful.

"I have also worked with a Strong Black Woman who possessed a no-nonsense, all-business persona. She was a working mother who raised two daughters by herself. While I liked her a lot, I'm not sure she was a person I ever got to know. It's important to let people know who you are (at least to some degree) if they are ever going to develop trust in you, not just your competencies. The most successful people in the world have mastered the art of relationship. Strong or otherwise, a big part of not having to do it all alone is your ability to allow the right people in your personal and professional life to come to your aid when needed. I have seen black women in the workplace struggle with the question of whom they could trust and whom they couldn't. They believe they can't afford to fail, so they try not to count on anyone but themselves. Unfortunately, this causes a lot of extra emotional and physical stress, which ultimately harms them and the people they love.

"When I started dating my wife, I became less of an outsider in my relationships with other black people. I was able to see the cost of strength in her life and the lives of other black women. I would like for my wife and for all black women to be able to continue to evolve because being strong is costing them dearly. My wife's coping abilities are so much different from (and in some respects better than) mine; but by the same token, I can't super-impose my own structure on her. Rather, I support her in doing whatever is necessary to defend her peace. As husband and wife, we both have obligations we must address collectively. So I can't say, 'Go do what ever you want. It doesn't matter.' But I can say, 'If you do this, what am I going to do?' Or, 'If I do this, what are you going to do?' Or 'What are we going to do?' At the end of the day the most important thing is that you be able to live with yourself as a black woman and as a human being.

"The conservatism of the black community in general is a problem for Strong Black Women. It gives them less room to cre-ate ideal scenarios for partnership. Strong Black Women are told what it means to be strong by the black community when in actu-ality they should spend more time tending to their own personal needs and desires. Communities are survival focused. They will change, stretch, grow, and contract in accordance with the forces that shape and influence them. Black women don't have to bear the burden of being the sole backbone of the black community. Until they lay that burden down, nobody else is going to have to come along and pick it up. Strength is a shared obligation. Men and women, blacks and whites, we all have a role in being strong for each other."

The New Strong, Black, and Balanced Woman

TERRELL HAILS FROM NASHVILLE, TENNESSEE, AND NOW DIVIDES his time between Harlem and Miami, Florida. He is thirty-five-years old, single, an English/liberal arts college graduate who works with kids as a teacher and is an artist in Harlem. Terrell is a gay black man.

"My mother is who comes to mind when I think of Strong Black Women. My mother, and all the women who have unconsciously become my friends because of her indelible mark on me, have given me a deep insight into the role of strength in these wom-en's lives. Strong Black Women do more than the average person should have to, and for the most part, they do it with a smile on their faces. The best parts of who I am becoming as a human being and as a man speak to what I want from my relationships with the Strong Black Women in my life.

"I have always believed that we are pure energy! What we give to the world is a direct output of our ability to call upon and balance our energy through the relationships we have in the world. There are two primary forms of energy that make up the duality in most living things. Life is set up to engage us as dual beings. Night and day, up and down, good and bad, yin and yang, and masculine and feminine are all forms of energy that live within each of us. As a man, and as a gay man in particular, I learn from the Strong Black Women in my life how to hone my own feminine energy. There is a level of giving that is unique to the feminine energy that Strong Black Women possess. It is beyond my general understanding as a masculine being. I believe it is a necessary trait in the context of creating a long-lasting relationship with a black man, and that is something that gay men and Strong Black Women have in common. By honing my femininity, I hope to create a balance of masculine/feminine energy within myself as a man for a successful and long-lasting relationship with another gay man.

"Three of my Strong Black Women friends have started referring to me as their 'girlfriend' in the past year. They have started calling me 'gurl.' I appreciate this because I want a level of communication and openness that will foster a more intimate level of relationship with the women I care about. I'm glad we can allow ourselves to let go of our own preconceived gender notions and have the kinds of personal exchanges that they might not necessarily get from a straight brother.

"I also desire and appreciate the continued nurturing I have always gotten from Strong Black Women. These sisters and I are kindred. They are Mother Earth–like and I love their wisdom and guidance. I am closer to these women than any man other than my father. They are different ages—thirty-eight, seventy, and ninety-five—and they are the three strongest black women I know and love. I want to be able to continue to love them….and trust them. I can use what they give me fully and freely, while with men, I have to weed out what they say and second guess their intentions.

"I guess I am a mama's boy, a responsible mama's boy but a mama's boy nonetheless. I say this because I love black women and recognize the need for positive and nurturing exchange between black men and women. Everything that these three women say or do to me shines with truth and love. Their level of wisdom is startling. They know who they are in strength and weakness. This level of personal power came through hard inner work and their willingness to release a lot of the cultural junk we pick up as black people in our society.

"I want my kindred sisters to always feel they can share their mistakes freely with me. They in turn are able to teach me how to be a Strong Black Man and, more importantly, to show me how to truly love black women. They show me how femininity can help me to better deal as a Strong Black Man with the women and men in my life by teaching me patience, forgiveness, and faith that God will order my steps. For these reasons and many more, the Strong Black Women in my life are priceless.

"I have also learned that endurance or putting up with a lot of crap from people doesn't necessarily guarantee inner peace in the lives of Strong Black Women. So I want them to do a better job of protecting their inner peace. I am always astonished at what black women are willing to endure from the men in their lives. All of the relationships they have with men are intimate even if they aren't sexual or romantic. However, seldom is their level of giving returned equally by the men in their lives. I want them to learn, as I have, to develop self-care. Self-care will allow them to feel they don't have to take on responsibilities that don't belong to them. They must learn to better prioritize who, where, and what to place their energy into and what to turn over to God's plan.

"I hope they will embrace a greater level of balance and permission to free themselves from doing many of the things that they have been taught to feel obligated to do. In doing so, they will learn, as I hope I have, to trust that things will take care of themselves, even if it is not as good or done in the way that I would have it. What happens will be the best that it can be given the experiences of those who stepped up to the plate and assumed responsibility. In essence, just give yourself permission to sit down every now and then. Stop feeding your need to care for everybody and be there through everything they go through in life.

"At seventy years of age, my dear friend Melanie had a wake-up call that helped her to realize she was not getting back what she had been giving in her relationship with a mutual friend. I love Melanie because she reminds me of Hannah or Ruth or Esther in the Bible. My nickname for her is Sojourner Truth. Unfortunately, her selfless care for others has resulted in her being lonely in relationships. What I mean by that is you can have a lot of people in your life and still feel lonely or misunderstood. This can happen easily when the only thing you do is give. People only get to know you as a giver, they only call upon you to give, and they only want you around when it is time to take from somebody (and usually that person is you).

"A few weeks ago, Melanie told me about a wake-up experience involving three mutual friends: Charlotte, Tim and Andy. Melanie has been a devoted friend of Tim's for more than twenty years. She has devoted a lot of her personal time and emotional energy to helping Tim embrace his personal truths as a black man, as a Christian man, and as a gay man. She has loved him unconditionally and has been there for him during times of duress and rejection by other friends, and even his family. In short, Melanie has been the one person whom Tim could always count on to tell him the truth about himself and who would hang around to help him conquer his personal demons.

"Meanwhile, Tim, who is in his sixties, has never learned to like himself, much less love himself. He hates growing older and is trying to act younger than his age. Tim is in love with Andy, another black gay man who is thirty years his junior and only pays attention to Tim when he needs something from him.

"Melanie and Tim were having dinner with Charlotte. Charlotte asked Tim, 'Who is your best friend?' Much to Melanie's shock and surprise, Tim responded, 'Andy.' I will never forget Melanie's voice as she told me how she felt at that moment. 'When he said Andy was his best friend, I nearly lost my breath! I thought of all of the times I have gone to the hospital with him, run errands for him, loaned him money, defended him in the presence of others, stood by his side! Child...this was a devastating wake up call. I have done everything for him out of love, not a sexual love but a deeper love.'

"Tim wasn't the first man who failed to appreciate Melanie for her caregiving qualities. Melanie was married for eighteen years. She woke up one morning and realized that she no longer needed her husband. He didn't bring anything to her life—financially, sexually, or emotionally—yet she had continued to give herself to him. After she had her wake-up call, she left him and has been alone ever since. More than anything, I want Melanie and all Strong Black Women to reclaim themselves. I want them to cultivate the self-care necessary to do for themselves what they have done consistently for others. I want them to practice being strong, black, and balanced women who embrace self-nurturing and self-worth, and who are as willing to receive as they are to give."

She Is My Inspiration

SINCE THEY WERE CHILDREN, JIMMY AND HIS SISTER CAROL HAVE both loved music. They grew up in a small town in North Carolina writing, singing, and performing music until finally, as young adults, they both set out to make names for themselves in New York City. Now Jimmy, a very highly respected, forty-year-old African-American songwriter, producer and artist, and Carol, a thirty-eight-year-old vocalist, producer, musician, and songwriter, have played with and written songs for some of the greatest names in show business. Jimmy was quick to tell me that he and Carol have a bond that is uncommon between siblings. It is because of this bond that Jimmy knows Carol, a Strong Black Woman, in a way that few others do.

"My sister, my mother, and her sisters are all Strong Black Women. I have witnessed them putting their minds to things and seen them manifest their goals. They are 'can-do' women. My mother and sister were the only two Strong Black Women

I knew growing up. They have both been an infinite source of inspiration in my life. My sister has been so much more than a sibling. She has been my motivator, my counselor, and my friend. She is a constant example in my life of how people should try to live their lives. She is disciplined and strong-willed. She is not afraid to work hard to achieve something, and she doesn't complain a lot while she is doing it. I am constantly reminded of the better person that I can become by watching and being with her. She is just a positive force in my life.

"Carol and I weren't close as kids, but when we both started working together in the music business we became inseparable. I cherish our relationship because we have each other as a support system. She supports me as a business colleague and as a sibling. She covers different parts of our business. Everything we both do is to help our company. We share the money we generate from our songwriting and music endeavors. We share responsibilities and we are constantly representing our company and each other unilaterally. Emotionally, she is a support system because she understands my passions, the choices I have made for my career, my struggles as a musician and as a man. I trust her instincts and her decision-making. As a Strong Black Woman, I can always count on Carol to do her part for the business.

"I want Carol to be happy and successful in her professional and personal life. She is pursuing solo music as a vocalist and she knows that she has my total support. I have seen her fight and overcome a lot of obstacles in her life. When producers said that she wasn't a good singer, she really worked hard to improve her voice. She was the valedictorian of her high school class. She has never been afraid to work hard. But the biggest display of her strength happened when she was diagnosed with breast cancer. Carol's career was going strong, she had just landed a great gig, and things were finally moving forward when she had what arguably was the biggest scare of her life. What amazed me is how Carol handled her diagnosis. She said, 'I am not going to take this lying down.' Carol did her research and found a doctor in Atlanta who was doing some experimental work using ancient herbal salves to treat breast cancer. She contacted the doctor and began self-administering the salve. The amazing thing is that Carol was diagnosed, treated, and is now cured from breast cancer while never muttering one word of complaint or missing a day of work. As always Carol was determined not to be proven wrong, even by breast cancer.

"I love my sister because of her strength. Even when she is giving me advice I don't like or necessarily want to hear, I know she is right. Not all family members can get along at the dinner table, much less in a business situation. I am a better person for having her as my sister, and I am lucky to be able to work with someone like her."

Making Sense of It All

A FEW YEARS AGO JOHN GRAY WROTE A VERY POPULAR BOOK TITLED *Men Are from Mars, Women Are from Venus,* which offered insights into the social and cultural differences between men and women. I refer to some of the principles presented in his book during many of the workshops I conduct on gender differences in the workplace. One day, while conducting a workshop on men and women as colleagues, it occurred to me that relationships are about more than the optimal matching and mixing of gender differences. Relationships in their most pure form are systems of self-actualization.

Men and women have been conditioned with many rules and regulations about the appropriate behaviors to display when interacting with members of the opposite sex. Furthermore, our culture rewards and penalizes us for how we behave in accordance to these socially prescribed rules. As people of color, our gender messages are further shaped by distorted racial notions about masculinity and femininity. With that much cultural pressure being placed on black men and women, it is no wonder many of us find it more and more difficult to take part in healthy relationships. It is no wonder that relationships generate more fear than joy for many people. It is also no wonder that on the first date we

bring along our boyfriend/girlfriend wish list, and on the second
date some of us are ready to rent a U-Haul.

Relationships aren't places where we lose or find ourselves. They
are places where we define and refine ourselves. Self-actualization
is a process of ongoing definition and refinement through the cultivation of healthy, open, loving, and honest interaction with others.
As I listened to the men and women I interviewed for this book, it
seemed to me that a lot of us have lost sight of the deeper value of
being in relationship.

Black Men in Pain

BLACK WOMEN KNOW THAT BLACK MEN ARE STILL IN A LOT OF PAIN.
I am not convinced that they know what is the best thing to do
about it. Their nurturing instincts as Strong Black Women kick
in, and before you know it, they have sacrificed their own self-
care in the effort to restore a black man (or men). While this is a
noble task, I am not convinced that this is always the best course
of action for black women. While black women are busy restoring
black men, it can send the wrong message to our black children,
that a woman's taking care of her man should take priority
over her taking care of herself, and her loving herself. I heard
countless versions of the "taking care of my man" story while
interviewing men and women for this book. In each, invariably
the Strong Black Woman ended up alone, unfulfilled, and bitter.
Then, when her hurt becomes anger, she is labeled as having a
bad attitude and shunned by men and women alike.

Strong Black Women must break this vicious emotional cycle
of self-destruction by allowing men to create their own tools and
resources for healing. Women can best support men in their healing by staying on the sidelines and cheering them on as they run
their emotional races. Doing so will challenge black men to create a greater sense of wholeness in their lives that isn't based on
the domination, disrespect, or abuse of women. Doing so means
black women will be able to devote more of their energies to taking care of themselves. And doing so means black women must
better learn the signs of a good man, what to do when they meet

a good man, and what to do when they meet a man who doesn't measure up.

AFFIRMATION

Today I will seek to fully understand the true intentions of the men in my life.

6 DATING WITH YOUR EYES WIDE OPEN: NEW RULES FOR AN OLD GAME (ROMANTIC, SELF)

*When self-respect takes its rightful place
in the psyche, you will not allow yourself to be
manipulated by anyone.* INDIRA MAHINDRA

HAVE YOU EVER RUSHED THROUGH THE SUPERMARKET AND IN your haste bought a bad piece of meat? Rather than taking the time to appropriately examine the meat, you grabbed the first piece of meat that "looked good" and zoomed home to throw it in the pan. Yes, my sisters, it is time to deal with why you choose the men you choose. I am sure that many of you have had a friend who, in her haste to find someone to love, continually dates partners who end up like that bad piece of meat at the supermarket. Some of us are better at reading the labels and checking the expiration date before we purchase a piece of meat than we are at heeding the warning signs that can appear in a new relationship. How effective are you at meeting, dating, and starting relationships with partners who will love, respect, and honor you?

The dating game for Strong Black Women is anything but a game. The stakes are high for black women looking for love. According to the U.S. Census Bureau, in 2000, 38 percent of black women ages eighteen and older had never married. In stark contrast, 18 percent of white women and 25 percent of Hispanic women within the same age category had never married. Simultaneous to the steady and marked decline in society's responsiveness to AIDS during the last decade, the face of AIDS in the United States of America has changed gender and race. The rate of HIV infection among African American women is four times higher than the rates among Latina women, and more than sixteen times higher than the rates among white women. Of newly HIV-infected women, 64 percent are African American. According to the Centers for Disease Control and Prevention, AIDS is the number-one killer for black American women between the ages of twenty-five and thirty-five.

To add economic weight to the condition of black women in America, according to a recent article in the NAACP's magazine, *The Crisis,* 86 percent of today's young black women are single when they have their first baby. Furthermore, in black families, 47 percent of children in single-parent homes live in poverty. This is where you really begin to feel the costs of being strong, black, and a woman in America.

In almost every way imaginable, black women are statistically at the bottom of the relationship totem pole. They are burdened with unique hurdles and challenges that women of other races and cultures experience to a lesser degree and with less serious consequences. A number of the women I interviewed while writing this book insisted that too many black women suffer as a result of their quest to find meaningful relationships with black men. A lot of the Strong Black Woman's condition is underscored by the plight of black men and black families in America.

According to *Minority Health Today,* the structure of the black family has undergone significant changes over the past thirty years. As the proportion of married black couples has declined, the proportion of divorced black couples has increased. Two-thirds of all black marriages end in divorce; two-thirds of black children experience the dissolution of their parents' marriage by the time they reach age sixteen.

The increased divorce rate among blacks has contributed to the challenges of being a Strong Black Woman in America. In 1970, 68 percent of black families featured a married, cohabiting husband and wife. This number dropped to just 50 percent in 1990, a decrease of 18 percentage points over 20 years, compared with a 6-percentage-point decrease over the same time period for white families. Black wives and husbands are also more likely to separate.

Many of the women I interviewed are hoping to build relationships with "good black men." Certainly a black man who can bring home a steady paycheck is an important part of that equation. But that consideration leads into another of the unique hurdles for women seeking relationships with black American men. According to Deborah Mathis, author of *Yet a Stranger: Why Black Americans Still Don't Feel at Home,* black professional men earn 21 percent less than similarly educated, experienced, and qualified white men. As a well-educated, professional black man who has worked hard to secure a successful career in corporate America, I have personally felt the pain that accompanies realizing I am not afforded equal pay for equal work because of the color of my skin. Lest you be fooled, the black women closest to me have shared in my pain. Women who date white men simply don't have to be strong for their men in this manner because of the unearned privilege afforded white men in the American workplace. It takes a lot to stand by your working black man when he is trying to survive a social system of exclusion that is bigger than him, and oftentimes invisible to every eye but his own. The black woman's recent rise up the corporate ladder can also create additional strain on black relationships. Some black men still feel threatened at the possibility of no longer being the primary revenue generator in the family.

Facing these challenges, how can a black woman remain optimistic about her prospects for partnership, family, and happiness? Rather than recognizing and heeding the signs of a "good man," some Strong Black Women make a potentially dangerous choice: to try to create the men of their dreams from the men in their lives at the moment. Strong Black Women can get typecast in one of two roles while trying to build a relationship with a black man in America. They can be labeled as *Makers of Men* or *Breakers of Men.*

Makers of Men

I HAVE KNOWN SEVERAL STRONG BLACK WOMEN WHO HAVE TRIED TO be Makers of Men. Rather than acknowledging the whole truth about a man, Makers of Men try to build relationships with men based on their perception of his potential to become her ideal partner. She believes she can improve upon an otherwise questionable choice of mate with a healthy dose of her tender loving care. This is a dangerous approach for a Strong Black Woman to take because it requires her to invest so much of her emotional energy and resources as a caregiver in this relationship.

Most Strong Black Women who identified themselves to me as Makers of Men reported that they seldom get to keep the men they set out to create. While some are quite skilled and resourceful at propping up their man, once the man is on his feet, he will often flee. With his newfound social value and personal pride, he sets out to experience the world as a new adventure, rather than stay with the woman and become the better, stronger, more caring, and more loving partner she desires.

Tiara, a thirty-five-year-old, college-educated, professional sister, fell in love with Carl, a twenty-eight-year-old black man who went to prison just two months after they met. She waited for him, provided emotional and financial support to him, and would not allow herself to consider dating another man for the entire year that her boyfriend was behind bars. "My girlfriends were ready to have me committed," she said later, reflecting back on this crazy, mixed-up time in her life. "Before meeting Carl, I had not had sex with a man in two years. Honey, for those two months the sex was great! I can admit it now, but back then I was just too desperate and needy to see the reality of my situation. I truly believed that if I waited on Carl, he would come out of jail and become the man I always dreamed of. We talked about the life we were going to create together during my prison visits. He was going to go back to school and then open a business, and I wanted to have kids. I really believed that all he needed was a Strong Black Woman at his side, and I was determined to be that woman. The truth is, I was aching for somebody to love me!

"I can say it now: basically Carl was a thug and I had fallen into thug love. As soon as he got his release, he disappeared."

A black woman's strength and determination can be a bad advisor when she is strongly feeling a particular lack in her life—especially if what she's lacking is love, warmth, sex, and companionship. Black women and men can be strong in one area of their lives while still being weak in others. When this happens, they can make unhealthy choices that bear great emotional consequences. Whether because they feel lonely, horny, or simply uncomfortable without a steady sexual and emotional relationship, some women simply close their eyes and hope that the first man who wants to spend time with them will also want to hang around the morning after.

Makers of Men, in their efforts to find love, can unwisely place themselves in circumstances that pose emotional (and sometimes even physical) danger. Secretly, they hope that if they are just sweet enough, generous enough, and sexy enough, the men they desire will stay around for a while. It is too easy to dismiss this as an issue only of black women's low self-esteem. Through their physical and emotional absence in the black family, men bear a large responsibility for how and why this happens. I believe that the craving for a loving and positive male figure in the life of a young black woman, when that woman was raised in a home where the father figure was physically or emotionally absent, can set her up to become a Maker of Men in her adult life.

Such was the case for Paula, a single, thirty-four-year-old, African American schoolteacher whose father abandoned her family when she was ten years old. "My last relationship ended a few months ago. It also represented the end of what had become a very unhappy and unsuccessful dating history. In short, I would say it was my wake-up call. I have had a history of picking men in need of a makeover, and Steven was the absolute worst of the lot.

"I met Steven one night at a club. I was standing outside having a cigarette and he walked up to me and started talking. Next thing I knew, we were back inside the club having a drink. It didn't take me long to realize that Steven didn't bring much to the table. He was unemployed and hadn't really done much with his life. He seemed nice enough, but there was a meanness that showed through even when he was trying to be charming. Sometimes when dating men, I let my emotions go numb. Even though I would see the writing on the wall, I would keep moving forward. I realize now how much I craved positive attention from a man. It reminds me of how I dealt with my parents' failing marriage when I was a child. Even though I knew things were bad between them, I hoped that if I was a good little girl (in other words, "strong" enough), Mom and Dad would want to work things out.

"One night after we had been dating for three months, Steven called to tell me that he had gotten into an argument with his cousin and had to move out immediately. I listened silently as he waited for me to extend an invitation to come and stay at my house. I remember thinking to myself as he was talking, 'Paula, don't do this to yourself. This is not going to work out.' As I suspected, he asked if he could stay with me for one month while he looked for work and his own place. I reluctantly said yes. Well, a month turned into six months of sheer hell and torment. I would come home from teaching school and find Steven sitting in the den watching television with his friends. He would pull his macho-man routine when they were at the house. He also did things to intimidate me and make me fear him. For example, after we had been living together for a month, he told me that he had served time in Desert Storm and was trained as a paratrooper and sniper. I didn't believe him, so he went upstairs to the bedroom, rifled through his suitcase, and came back downstairs with a gun in his hand. I freaked out since I have always been afraid of guns. It was like he was showing me the gun as a warning to not mess with him.

"Shortly after that night, we started arguing over silly things. A few times in the heat of an argument, he grabbed me around the neck and pushed me up against the wall. He would manhandle me when he wanted to make a point or when I caught him in a lie. I had been abused before by men, though most of it was verbal abuse. His physical aggressiveness scared me. By the end of the second month we were sleeping in separate bedrooms in my house. I kept my bedroom door locked at night because I was afraid of him.

"You know, I understand now why wives poison their husbands. You cook for them and care for them, and all you get in return is abuse. Steven's abuse and disrespect got so bad that I started spending nights at my girlfriend's house. After a few more months, I got him to agree on a move-out date, which he first said was going to be Thanksgiving, and then later pushed out to the end of the year. I tried to get a restraining order to remove him from my house. When I went to the police, they told me that since he was a tenant in my house and I wasn't his wife, they were not able to help me. They told me that I could get a restraining order only after he had harmed me. So, I tried to get a male relative to temporarily move into the house with me. No such luck. I was stuck with this man in my house. I was afraid to be in the house with him, and I was even more afraid to force him to leave against his will.

"On January 2, I changed the locks to my house. Finally, Steven was gone from my home and my life. At the strong urging of my mother, whose wise counsel regarding Steven I had ignored previously, I decided to seek out the help of a therapist. I have always considered myself to be a strong woman. I worked my way through college, I own my own home, and I am very independent, but in other ways, I didn't take care of myself. I needed to look at why I was selecting men who couldn't contribute to my life. Therapy has been the greatest gift I have ever given myself. I am learning how to date while honoring a deeper level of self-care. I am also paying attention to the relationship warning flags that I had ignored in past."

Equal or Not?

EVERY STRONG BLACK WOMAN I HAVE EVER MET HAS HER OWN UN-forgettable style. She has a stride about her that simply cannot be imitated. Some are brash, loud, and sassy, while others are silent, observant, and enchanting. No matter the style, they created it, they own it, and they take it everywhere they go, even into their romantic encounters. As Strong Black Women I interviewed frequently shared with me, men can sometimes feel threatened by their uncompromising style. On the one hand, men say they like a woman who is not afraid to go after what she wants and who has her own independent life. They say they welcome a confident, go-get-it kind of woman who can handle herself in any situation.

They will even say they want a woman who is intelligent, who speaks her mind, and who is their peer. But many men become threatened when they meet a woman who possesses all of these stated desirable qualities because, in essence, they don't feel as needed or as valued as a man. Consequently, many Strong Black Women get kicked to the curb because of the very qualities that men say they find attractive about them. They are told they are too strong, that they should be more agreeable, or even that they act like they want to be the man in the relationship. When a Strong Black Woman's character and femininity are attacked, it can be especially damaging and confusing.

In Strong Black Women's attempts to simply be themselves, they are often unfairly accused of challenging a brother's manhood. They do this through their unwillingness to surrender themselves to what some black men see as the natural, God-inspired, superior role of a man in relationship to a woman. As Michael mentioned in chapter five, "marriage [or a relationship] is a corporation. A corporation can only have one CEO, and I was raised to believe that the husband is the CEO." While not all Strong Black Women are categorically opposed to a black man operating as CEO of the relationship or marriage, they are not and should not be willing to assume anything less than the chief operating officer (COO) position. In the business world, competitive organizations are run by strong, collaborative leadership teams. In other words, two heads are better than one. This goes both for realizing competitive advantage in today's business world and for sustaining healthy, loving, vital relationships. In effective organizations, decisions are made by consensus and based upon the organization's vision, mission, strategy, and current business imperatives. Likewise, for a relationship to grow and become stronger, the man and woman must share a united vision and equal voice in the relationship. Furthermore, they must define a mission to live by, set a strategy to achieve their goals, and communicate life's challenges and opportunities to each other in a manner that supports the highest purpose of their relationship.

When a woman defines and defends her role as COO, she is not attempting to break her man; rather, she is attempting to demonstrate her commitment to the relationship as a full and equal partner. Being a full and equal partner means that both the man and the woman have *equal power* over the decisions and actions they make as a couple. From this place, they can openly and honestly make sacrifices and decisions that they won't silently regret later. It also means that they have a responsibility to behave in a manner that supports the well-being of both the relationship and of each other. When a man expects his mate to assume the role of office manager rather than COO of the relationship, he is minimizing her contribution and power in the relationship.

Left Standing on the Dance Floor

RACHEL IS A SISTER WHO HAS IT ALL GOING ON. WHILE SHE COMES from a background of abandonment and abuse, she has risen above those challenges and worked diligently to become the kind of woman she has always wanted to be. Now in her early fifties, Rachel is divorced, a mother of a grown son, a thirty-year cancer survivor, and a thriving corporate professional who is at the top of her game and loving it. She rose above the adversity in her life by embracing herself and not putting up with what she calls "life's bullshit." Recently Rachel was being courted by a prominent, well-heeled professional in her community—a tall, dark, and handsome brother in his mid-fifties who lost his wife a year and a half earlier. He met her briefly on several occasions at a few choice social events around town. He reached out to make contact with Rachel through a mutual friend and Rachel responded to his advances, in her usual style.

"I should have followed my first mind. However, what caused me to allow him to pursue me was that he possessed a lot of qualities that are attractive to me. He was good-looking, I mean *really* good-looking. He was in the world of high finance and did million dollar deals. He was absolutely charming and was well known in our community. I could take him to any social function, and he was as much of a social butterfly as I am. We both loved jazz, we were both world travelers, and we both love fine foods. And we looked good together. So I said, OK, I will give this a shot.

"Now, from the very start I noticed behaviors that I wrote off as nothing more than his little quirks. After all, he was married thirty years, recently widowed, and was just starting to date again. He was a black man who was raised in a very traditional, South American, male-dominated culture. But from the start he was overly sensitive about silly-ass things and he was quick to let his ego rule him. Well child...before long those damn little quirks became big fucking loopholes! They turned into caverns! They weren't little bumps, they weren't a scratch in the record, they were caverns and caves filled with deep, dark-ass secrets that screamed out FOOL!

"For example, I teased him one day and asked him if he wanted to be my arm candy. At first he didn't know what I was talking about. When I explained it to him, he recoiled and said, 'absolutely not.' Now, I know I make damn good arm candy. I am attractive, intelligent, successful, and a fun woman to be with. But I realized that when he said he wanted to meet someone who he could love and take care of and get the same thing in return, he secretly had a very different notion in mind than me. You see, in every way I was truly his peer. On the other hand, his dearly departed was just his wife. So while he said he wanted a woman like me, he wanted me to become something that I was not meant to be. The interesting part about him was that at first I found it very charming that he referred to his deceased wife as his partner. He would tell me that she was his 'partner in every way.' In reality he was the boss and she was his executive secretary. She lived by his law, on his terms, and under his rule. It took me a while to figure this out, but on one of our dates, this point was made clear for me.

"He called to invite me to dinner and a jazz club to see an artist I had seen a million times before. I had a photo shoot the next day and had to prepare to leave town. Early that afternoon he called to say that the show started at 9:00 p.m. and that he wanted to pick me up at 6:00 p.m. so we could have dinner at the jazz club before the show. I said that sounds good, but since the jazz club is located in the restaurant district, let's pick another restaurant for dinner since the food at the jazz club is not that great. All of a sudden there was a pregnant pause. Now I caught his pause, but I kinda didn't catch the real meaning of the pause. I thought that he was just thinking things over because he is a very analytical and nonspontaneous person. So I told him that I would continue preparing for my trip and call him later to let him know if I would be able to make it that evening. After about forty minutes, I realized that I didn't really want to go out to dinner and a show since I had to leave first thing in the morning, so I called him back. I told him that I wanted to take a raincheck because I was too behind on my work and I needed to be totally prepared for my business trip the next day. He said, 'No problem, Rachel, no problem, but let me share something with you.' I said sure. I thought he was going to share a packing tip or a travel tip. Instead he said in a stern but polite tone, 'When a gentleman invites you to dinner, never tell him that the restaurant he has selected to take you to doesn't serve food that is good enough for you to eat.' I said, 'Whoa! Wait a minute. I never said that the food wasn't good enough for me, I said that the food they serve does not taste that good. My dear, you have issues about every little thing. You are too sensitive. This is not working. If I can't even tell you that the food at a restaurant is not that good, then we need to leave this alone. Now, I gotta go.' I hung up the phone because I just didn't want to deal with his silly-ass drama. However, now I had another problem on my hands. I had already invited him to the Arts Ball in two weeks.

"So I called my girlfriend and told her what happened. She said 'That Negro is crazy! You need to leave him alone!' I agreed and said I needed to find a way to rescind his invitation to the Arts Ball. I left the next morning for my eight-day business trip and never gave him a second thought. When I returned home, I decided to call him. Surprisingly, he was very happy to hear from me. Beaming, he said, 'Hi Rachel, it is so good to hear from you. How are you? I haven't heard from you in a while. Have you been traveling?' We exchanged charming pleasantries, and I ended up asking him if he had plans for dinner the next day. He replied that he was free. All of a sudden he began to open up. He told me that he had turned down several invitations because he was still going through a lot with the loss of his wife and, even more recently, his mother. He also had an estranged relationship with his daughter. I told him that I was going to a mutual friend's house for dinner the next night. Much to my surprise, he said that he would love to join me. I said, 'OK, great, why don't you pick me up about 7:15 tomorrow night.' Once again there was his silence. I heard the silence and said, 'What is it?' He said, 'Well, you obviously don't know me yet.' Then I said, 'Well what is there to know? I asked you to pick me up at 7:15 p.m. What is there to know?' Then he said, 'Obviously this is a getting-to-know-you process. Time will tell. I ask you to please be patient with me.' I said, 'No problem.'

"He shows up the next day at my house. I drove us to dinner, which was different for him. He commented that it felt strange being driven by a woman on a date. Much to my surprise, we had a wonderful evening both during dinner and during the drive back home. Since we had such a good time that evening, I decided to invite him to Thanksgiving dinner the next day. Before he answered, he asked me if I was preparing Thanksgiving dinner for him. Then after I said no, I was preparing dinner for my son and grandchild, he declined and said that was too much for him. I thought to myself, 'whateva!'

"Well, since we had such a good time at dinner the week before, I decided to go ahead and have him escort me to the Arts Ball. Now I was learning how to handle some of his little quirks. This time I decided not to call him and tell him what time to pick me up for the Ball. Instead, I let him handle it. Sure enough, he called and told me to be ready by 6:00 p.m. I made sure that I was ready and fabulous when he arrived at 6:00 p.m. I even had champagne chilled so we could share a toast before we headed to the Ball. From the time we arrived at the Ball, people were stopping us to tell us how great we looked together. When we went to the reception table to pick up the place cards I noticed him wince. The place cards only had my name and 'guest.' Hey, I am a busy girl! I forgot to call and give them his name!

"As the evening proceeded, we both walked around the room to see who was there. We walked to one side of the room where he wanted to introduce me to all the people with old money. Laughing, I replied that the people with the real money were sitting at my table on the other side of the room, and I knew them all personally. After meeting and greeting his business associates and friends, we headed to the dance floor. We danced and laughed, and danced some more. All eyes were on us because were cutting a rug on the dance floor.

"After about twenty minutes on the dance floor, I said to him, 'Come on, let's go see what is happening over there.' As I turned away from him to head in the direction that I had mentioned, he grabbed my arm and pulled me back toward him. He said, 'Let me tell you something! When you are with me, you are with me! You cannot do what you want to do!' After I recovered from the shock of his actions, I put a big smile on my face so as not to create a scene and I said, 'I am not your damn child! I am a grown-up woman. I do what I want to do!' He huffed and puffed and said, 'Then if you are going to do what you want to do, you don't need me. I think you should find a ride home with one of your friends. You don't need me!' With a smile still on my face I told him, 'I don't need to find a ride home because I followed my first mind and brought along my cab fare in case you decided to act a fool.' With that, Mister Tall, Dark, and Handsome stormed off the dance floor and left me standing there.

"Well, what did I learn from this experience? First of all, always follow your first mind. If it walks, quacks, and acts like a duck, run in the other direction. I saw the signs that he was not the man for me early on in the dating game. But I was captured by his ability to fulfill so many of the boxes on my ideal-man checklist. Sometimes as a Strong Black Woman, you try to make a square peg fit a round hole. In his mind I was trying to challenge his position as a man. He felt that I was trying to train him, so he tried to train me.

"Second, I don't know that I should have done anything different in this situation. I do know that I will not let this situation dictate what my next dating experience will be. A lot of sisters bring unreleased baggage from their dating and relationship history along on their next date. I try really hard not to do that.

I still believe that there are some good men out here and eventually I will meet one, but maybe I won't. No matter what, I won't let anyone steal my rhythm or change my groove.

"Third, while I am not trying to break a man, I will not allow myself to be broken. There are trade-offs that you make in any relationship, but I will not let my spirit be muted. In the end it is all I have. A lot of men are attracted to Strong Black Women because of our sassy ways. They say that they want a Strong Black Woman and then when they get one, they try to put her on remote control. Well, you can't turn me on when you want me on, and turn me off when you want me off.

"Finally, while I am waiting for the right man to come along, I am going to stay busy, make myself happy, and continue working on my mind, body, and soul. That way if and when I meet him, I will be prepared. Until then, I am just going to keep on dancing!"

Clearly Tiara, Paula, and Rachel's experiences don't represent the sum total of dating experiences for all Strong Black Women. However, many stories go untold about how the consequences of dating with your eyes shut continue to affect women of color everywhere. One of the most drastic consequences of not embracing a philosophy and practice of self-care while dating is when, in a moment of blindness, you make assumptions about a lover that cost you your health and quality of life. Such was the case for Marisol, a forty-five-year-old Latina from California who met the man of her dreams and fell in love. He gave her a son—and he infected her with the HIV virus, which she has lived with for the past nineteen years. Now she is a single mother, an AIDS activist, and is on disability while she focuses on her own self-care. She offered the following advice on self-care for women who date with their eyes shut.

The Down-Low (DL) Dilemma

"I WAS YOUNG AND NAIVE. MY SON'S FATHER WAS A GOOD MAN, BUT I didn't know his whole story. When I met him, I assumed that he was heterosexual. He was a very handsome, well-educated, professional man. We were very attracted to each other and I trusted him. During those days, AIDS was new for everybody. We thought of it as a disease that could only be contracted by a very small segment of the population, gay men. Never in a million years did I ever think that I could contract HIV. Nor did I think that my son's father was sleeping with anybody else but me, much less other men. In reality, he was living a double life, on the down-low. I never even asked him about his past relationships, because in my culture that is considered a person's private affair. Eventually, he admitted that while he had slept with other men when he was sexually active with me, he still didn't consider himself to be gay. I, like a lot of young women, didn't know how to talk about sexuality and sexual history with men. Even if we have our suspicions about the sexual orientation of a mate, many prefer to turn their heads. We don't want to turn our men off or seem too pushy, so we don't ask. Instead, we just close our eyes and hope that the man of our affection will love, care for, and protect us.

"Over the years, I've learned that bisexuality is more tolerated in situations where women sleep with members of both sexes than with men who sleep with members of both sexes. Bisexual men live in an awkward place between the straight world and the gay world. As straight women, we have not been sympathetic to their unique circumstances, much less in their corner. I remember the comments of many straight women when AIDS first became known as a homosexual disease. We pointed our fingers and blamed the victim. We didn't stand by our sons, brothers, fathers, and lovers. Instead, many of us said it was God's redemptive plan for them. Today we want these men to trust us enough to be open and honest about the inner workings of their sexuality. But black men and women haven't worked hard enough to lay the groundwork of trust and non-judgment necessary to facilitate a loving exchange about sexuality, especially bisexuality. Now that the down-low man's crisis has become ours, some of us think that the most important course of action we can take is to hold their feet to the fire for causing our health crisis and risking our demise.

"When do we start talking about why black women and men more often than not refuse to fully disclose their sexual history and current practices? When do we start talking about what we need to do as women and men to create a safe space in our relationships to fully express and share our sexuality, orientations, and desires? Why is it easier for some of us to continue pointing the finger at them rather than empowering ourselves with the responsibility for our own physical, emotional, and sexual well-being? It seems to me that we are highlighting the symptom, not the problem. The symptom is the rising transmission of the HIV virus between men and women in communities of color without their knowledge or attention. The illness is that our deeply rooted homophobia and internalized homophobia is what has been placing the Hispanic and black family at risk long before the advent of HIV. It attacks our relationships between mother and child long before it infects our bodies.

"How can we expect men who continue to be discriminated against because of their sexual orientation to take our best interests to heart when we allow them (unknowingly perhaps) to lie down with us? Being in the closet or on the DL is an act of self-preservation for many men who otherwise fear the consequences of living life out of the closet. I know this is true because I saw what coming out of the closet cost my son's father.

"In many ways, I believe we are more tolerant of the stereotypical gay man who is out of the closet and therefore open about his sexual practices, than of fearful men who are still in the closet or live their lives on the DL. It is very easy to blame bisexual men for not being forthcoming about their sexual practices because it stops us from taking our responsibility in the dating process to collect and share the information necessary to protect ourselves while dating. This is not about placing blame; it is about avoiding foolish mistakes in your quest to find love and companionship. Today I am living with AIDS, raising my son as a single parent, and trying to find my way in the world with the help of friends and family. I don't think we can afford to waste any more time pointing fingers and placing blame on men on the DL for our physical condition and safety. Doing so is not solving the problem, rather it is driving us further at odds. My son's father was a very good man. He was smart, talented, and a successful and well-respected professional. I wanted my son to have a positive, honest, and healthy relationship with his father, so I had to release my anger in the hopes of making the most of this unfortunate situation.

"What I have learned is that we are all targets of homophobia. Both my son's father and I have suffered as victims of internalized homophobia and homophobia. I decided to examine my own homophobia because I didn't want to put my son at risk of being blinded by homophobia. He loves me, he had a positive relationship with his father, and most importantly, he is growing into a whole, healthy, and honest young man. His father is gone now, but my son has no regrets toward me because I cultivated a loving and honest relationship with his father. I saw this as my responsibility because my son is all I have.

"I want women of color to start taking greater responsibility for their emotional and physical health while finding love. You can start by practicing open and honest communication and asking the right questions before you have intercourse. Believe me, the questions you don't ask today can hurt you."

From Me to You with Love and Concern

As a man who loves and cares about Strong Black Women, I agree with Marisol: ask the tough questions of your lover. First and foremost, before you sleep with anyone, both of you should take an HIV test. Purchase a home-testing kit in anticipation of that magic moment. If your lover is not willing to take the test, I am gonna tell you like I would tell a daughter, sister, niece, or any other beloved woman in my family, Don't take a foolish chance! Close your legs and leave him alone! For the record, I tell the young men in my family, "If you have decided to be sexually active, care enough about yourself and your partner to cover it up. You have too much to live for."

Now, just because you have gotten your man to take an HIV test doesn't mean that it is OK to have unprotected sex with him. Unless you are with your lover twenty-four hours a day and you know each other's every move in life, you must consider the real possibility that he or she could contract the HIV virus from someone else. If you truly care for each other, then you would not want to do anything that would put your lover or yourself at risk. However, as the statistics illustrate, black women in America (most of whom are single) and around the world are not doing everything within their personal power to protect themselves from HIV exposure. The reason I hear most often for this lack of self-responsibility and self-care is, "My man says using a condom detracts from the pleasure of having sex." When you hear this from a man, delete him from your cell phone, remove him from your Rolodex, and trust me when I say he is not a man who is going to love, protect, and cherish you. Your life is worth more than his orgasm, or yours for that matter.

While it is helpful to know a person's sexual history for any number of reasons, just because your lover has shared intimate details about his sexual past doesn't mean that you know the whole story. How many times have you volunteered the secret details of your past relationships with someone who you are still getting to know, trust, and potentially love? Remember what Darryl said in chapter five: "Women talk, so I have learned that any time I interact with a sister, my masculinity is being broadcast to the world." This belief drives a lot of the behaviors that men—whether straight, bisexual, or gay—demonstrate in their relationships. Regardless of a man's sexual orientation, his sexual identity is just as important to him as your femininity is to you. I have straight male friends who have been accused of not being straight enough and I have gay male friends who have been accused of not being gay enough. We are all susceptible to the judgments and stereotypes of our peers. Consequently, many men are very cautious about sharing any controversial aspects of their sexual history or sexuality. It is simply too risky for them.

Given the risks and realities of dating today, Strong Black Women have to protect themselves physically and emotionally. Insisting on safe sex is the best way to physically protect yourself from the potential physical hazards of dating. But women also have to do what they need to do to protect themselves emotionally while not violating their lovers' sense of safety and privacy.

This can be as challenging as mustering up the strength to take an HIV test with your lover.

There are parts of our individual life histories that all of us will likely carry to our graves without telling anyone. Since you can't rely on a lover to give honest answers to all of your inquiries into his sexual past or present, you must invest the effort to create and honor trust in your relationship. This happens best by encouraging lots of open, non-judgmental conversation and sharing about sex, intimacy, and sexuality—something that many black women and men find difficult to do. Once a man completely trusts a woman, and feels safe letting his guard down, he is much more likely to share his vulnerabilities with you. Cherish his confidences, because a trustworthy woman is sexy in the eyes of any lover man.

The Five Signs of a Good Man

FINALLY, I ASKED MANY OF THE MEN I INTERVIEWED FOR THIS BOOK what they believed were the signs of a good man. They offered the following signs as a way for women to know whether the men in their romantic and platonic lives are keepers or losers.

He knows your value. Men know when a woman doesn't love herself and some of them will take advantage of it. A recent research study performed with 188 male and female teenagers ages twelve to fourteen illustrated this very point when it examined the link between self-esteem and virginity. Researchers found that girls who had high self-esteem were three times more likely to have remained virgins compared with girls who had low self-esteem. On the other hand, boys with high self-esteem were 2.4 times more likely to have initiated intercourse than those with low self-esteem. By knowing your value and practicing self-care, you protect and strengthen your self-esteem. Once a man is clear about how you feel about yourself, he will treat you accordingly. Your level of self-care shows him what you will accept from him and what you will not accept from him as a lover and as a friend. In short, by knowing and cherishing your value, you set the standard for your relationship. One more thing—one of the

men I interviewed offered the following warning to Strong Black
Women: "Just because the sex is good between you and your man
doesn't mean you should take a lot of shit from him. Once you head
down this road, you have lost any chance for lasting happiness."

He must be honest above all else. The men I interviewed all
said that an honest man is a good man. If you meet a man who
is willing to put everything out on the table, give him a second
look. It is essential that an honest man's words match his actions. If he tells you that he does not drink and every Friday
night he is hanging out at a club with the fellas, chances are you
have a problem. Sometimes a man who is honest about the big
things in your relationship will lie about the little things. It is
his way of keeping the peace. But be careful: if your man feels
the need to dodge the truth, then he doesn't feel he can totally
trust himself in your relationship. Make sure that you identify
and discuss half-truths with your man, and if they keep showing up, take heed. A good man has nothing to hide and will be
honest in his relationship with you because he wants and needs
your honesty in return.

He can turn his dreams into reality. A man's potential is what
he has when he isn't doing anything. If your man is full of dreams
but has not created a game plan, take note. If he is more interested in complaining about why he can't do what he is meant to
do, watch out. A good man is a man who is ready, willing, and able
to turn his dream into a reality. A lot of brothers have dreams but
lack the ability to realize them. They can have a million reasons
and people to blame for their unrealized dreams. Make sure that
you believe in his dreams, but let them remain his dreams, for
him to manifest. Don't try to use your strength to realize them for
him. If you do, you might live to regret it. Likewise, if you meet a
brother who is afraid to dream, he is not ready to have a Strong
Black Woman at his side. You will only make him realize how
powerless he is over his own life as you try to go about realizing
your own dreams.

He can tell you when he is hurt. Men who don't practice emotional self-care themselves find it difficult to communicate the
unresolved and unreleased hurt in their lives. I don't care how

tough a man is: *all* men are full of emotions that are searching for a way to be expressed. What matters is a man's ability to channel the hurt he experiences in life in a positive and healing direction. If you meet a man who cannot tell you when he is hurt, pay attention. Men who are abusive or prone to emotional and physical abandonment are typically men who are not able to deal with the hurt that has accumulated in their lives. As a result, their interpersonal interactions with other men and women can trigger pain and disable them from being emotionally available.

He embodies compassion How does your man treat other people? Is he the kind of man who complains during dinner out on the town and then doesn't leave the waiter a tip? Does he routinely cut people off while driving? Is he generally rude to customer service people and strangers? Is he the kind of man who smiles easily when he meets your friends or colleagues? Does he listen and give you his undivided attention when you are having a conversation? Does he check out other women on the sly when he is in your presence? Is he able to see both sides of a sticky situation? Does he use terms that disrespect gender, race, nationality, religion, or sexual orientation? When you spend time together, does he ask you how you would like to spend the afternoon together? Is he patient with you when you are having a bad day? Does he care about and take time to remember the little things? When you add up your answers to all of these questions, you can begin to see if your man is the kind of person who has high, medium, or low consideration for the well-being of his fellow humans. Men who lack compassion tend to have a lower capacity to care for others, and in time that may include you.

Keep Your Eyes Open

IN THIS CHAPTER, I WANTED TO SHARE WITH YOU SOME OF THE STO-ries of women who used to date with their eyes shut, and who now, after healing their emotional blind spots, feel better prepared to choose and participate in relationships with their eyes wide open. There are many variables in the wild world of dating and relationships that are out of the control of any individual black woman.

Keeping your eyes wide open doesn't mean that you must keep a suspicious lookout for the hidden faults in a potential mate. It also doesn't mean that you must keep up a strong armor, or use trickery to uncover the secret intentions of that new special someone in your life. Doing these things only ensures that you will find what you seek and miss the rest.

Rather, keeping your eyes wide open means learning to look beyond the surface of your own desires and fears, and the stated desires of your new love interest. It means taking things slowly. Over time you will distinguish between your fears, your feelings, and your instincts about a new relationship. Acknowledge your feelings, release your fears, and cultivate your instincts. Heed the signs that indicate danger on the horizon.

I have watched a lot of women be strong in their relationships with men. They put up with their man's nonsense, they tolerate his indiscretions, and they endure his pain. They do this to keep the relationship alive, but they sacrifice their own personal power and self-care in the process. You must cultivate and defend self-care within each of your relationships if you want to maintain healthy, loving, and supportive interactions with your loved ones. By doing this you will become like a bright light. Now, bright lights still attract flies, but they also light the way for those in search of the real thing. When you embrace your own self-care, you can shoo away the flies and let the world know that you are the real thing.

AFFIRMATION

*Today I will embrace the opportunity to see
beyond the clouds of my fears and frustrations,
to celebrate the truth in my relationships,
and to follow the wisdom of my heart.*

7 TRANSCENDING SILENCE: STRAIGHT AND LESBIAN SISTERS TALK (PLATONIC, SELF)

*In the same way that the existence of the self-defined
black woman is no threat to the self-defined black man,
the black lesbian is an emotional threat only to those
black women whose feelings of kinship and love for other
black women are problematic in some way.* AUDRE LORDE

YOLANDA AND KAREN BECAME BEST FRIENDS AFTER MEETING
in an advanced-placement English course in high school. All
throughout their high school years they were inseparable. They
did everything together—shared clothes and make-up tips, talked
about boys, and even promised to be maid of honor at each other's
weddings. As time passed they grew into young women and continued to support each other as best friends do. Yolanda stood by
her side after Karen was date-raped in college. Karen was the loving rock of strength when Yolanda lost her mother to cancer. When
Karen met and married the man of her dreams, Yolanda stood by
her side as maid of honor, just as she had promised many years
earlier. It seemed as if nothing could come between them—until
the day that Yolanda told Karen that she was a lesbian.

It seems that there is never more mistrust between black
women than when it comes to the gender of the people you share
your bed with. Even if they are openly accepting of their gay male
friends, many—but not all—heterosexual black women strongly
oppose the notion that they can befriend and trust a black lesbian. Likewise, many black lesbians firmly oppose any dem-
onstration of friendship and sisterhood with black women who
sleep with men. The lack of dialogue and camaraderie between
straight, bisexual, and lesbian black women prompted me to talk
to Strong Black Women of diverse sexual orientations about what
they would like each other to stop, start, and continue doing in

order to promote greater sisterhood among black women of all sexual orientations.

Regardless of sexual orientation, family values, or religious beliefs, Strong Black Women should never forget that we all live in a made-for-men world. As the most racially and sexually maligned group of people in America, black women of all sexual identities must fight to eliminate any self-imposed attitudes or behaviors that further marginalize their status in our society. To do so, black men and women must stop, look, and listen to the ways we exclude each other because of sexism and homophobia.

Silence and Invisibility

SILENCE, MISREPRESENTATION, AND INVISIBILITY ARE THE THREE most oppressive forces facing black women in America today. If you don't believe me, just flip through the pages of America's top-selling weekly magazines and newspapers and pull out the images of black women. Do you honestly think that these images fully and accurately reflect the depth, breadth, and diversity of black women in America?

The root of silence and invisibility in any relationship is fear. As black people in America, we are taught to fear many things, but especially difference. We are taught that difference will hurt us. We fear the differences that exist among us more than we fear the differences we encounter among people not of our complexion and gender. This fear of our own diversity derails us from fully embracing ourselves. Until black women and men of all sexual orientations embrace change, we will not create values, beliefs, and family systems that celebrate our diversity, and all the advantages that diversity brings with it. Black people are still too bound to the belief that if you are not like me, than I must be against you.

We come from an ancestral history that embraced our uniqueness and celebrated many forms of black-on-black relationships. In *Sister Outsider,* Audre Lorde points to an interesting aspect of African culture that created space in the African family system for a breadth of inclusive, loving relationships: "On the West Coast of Africa, the Fon of Dahomey still have twelve different kinds of marriage. One of them is known as 'giving the goat to the buck,' where a woman of independent means marries another woman who then may or may not bear children, all of whom will belong to the bloodline of the first woman. Some marriages of this kind are arranged to provide heirs for women of means who wish to remain 'free,' and some are lesbian relationships. Marriages like these occur throughout Africa, in several different places among different peoples. Routinely, the women involved are accepted members of their communities, evaluated not by their sexuality but by their respective places within the community."

Both black and White America have historically entrusted their children to the safe bosom of black women. However, when black women exclude each other and treat their differences as impassable roadblocks, that same black bosom becomes unsafe for its own mothers, daughters, sisters and friends.

The women I interviewed talked in a very open and frank manner about the fears, hopes, struggles, and successes they have experienced in creating platonic, loving relationships among straight, bisexual, and lesbian black women. They also shared some of the attitudes, reactions, and behaviors that they believe black women can adopt to become more accepting of women of all sexual identities. Black women, both straight and lesbian, offered very specific suggestions for enhancing sisterhood across lines of sexual orientation. I was surprised to learn that while the perspectives of straight and lesbian black women are distinctive, the changes they are seeking from each other are very similar. Creating new and more inclusive emotional spaces is the only way that black people can transcend the silence that endangers sisterhood in black America.

Lesbian Sisters' Requests of their Straight Black Sisters

Request #1: **Stop thinking that all lesbians are the same, because it stereotypes us and makes it difficult for you to get to know us better.**

Non-blacks have hurled a lot of arrows at black Americans because of our physical appearance. We have been accused of everything from looking like primates to having tails. We've suffered centuries of foul race-based stereotypes founded on our physical and cultural characteristics. Have you ever been told by another black person that you don't sound or act black, or that you dress like a white girl? These are painful words to hear, especially when they come from the mouths of people who share your hue and your history.

Black lesbians and gay men today are even more besieged by arrows hurled at them by their own black sisters and brothers because they don't look or act straight. Likewise, black lesbians and gay men experience another level of stereotyping within the black community that denies them the right to fully express themselves for fear they will be labeled with terms like "bull dyke," "faggot," or worse. One straight black woman I interviewed openly admitted her fear about her less feminine black lesbian sisters: "I must admit that when a lesbian is really butch-acting and -looking, I become wary of getting to know her. I know that I shouldn't judge a book by its cover, but then again, birds of a feather flock together. I don't want anybody getting the wrong idea about me."

Jacquelyn, a twenty-four-year-old black bisexual woman who lives in Oakland, echoed the sentiments of many of the lesbian and bisexual women I spoke with about the problem of stereotypes when it comes to building relationships with straight black women. "I am a biracial and bisexual army brat," she said. "My father is black American and my mother is German. Growing up with parents who lived outside of the United States had a profound impact on my identity as a Strong Black Woman and as a sexual being. A lot of my African American girlfriends—both straight and lesbian—tend to have a strong need to place themselves and others into tightly sealed identity boxes. That just doesn't work for me. So when the topic of who you are sleeping with comes up, I tend to respond by saying, 'I am a switch-hitter! I have probably slept with more women than most of my lesbian friends and more men than most of my straight friends! So what does that make me?'" Laughing, she went on, "A ho? For God's sake, when do the stereotypes end? Straight or gay, we all place these stereotypes on each other so that we can judge ourselves and our sisters. But how does it really benefit you if you only see me as you want to see me? You will always blind yourself to the real me.

"As a femme, bisexual, Strong Black Woman, I make both men and women uncomfortable. Being bisexual challenges the often-unchallenged belief that straight and gay orientations are mutually exclusive and opposing identities. In other words, if I am straight am I more likely to sleep with or love a man simply because he is a man? Not! Likewise, if I am a lesbian, am I only capable of loving and being satisfied by a woman? Pleeeze! I think it is all a bunch of bullshit—even more bullshit than we feed each other about the mind-fuck condition we call race. I select my partners based on their inner qualities, not what the white male heterosexual's oppressive Bible says, and not by some mismatched need to be stamped and approved by this patriarchal, hedonistic, and multiculturally truncated society.

"Some men think that I am bisexual simply because I haven't been 'taken care of' by the right man. These weenie-wacked fools think they are the right men that can turn me around and get me on the straight track. Gimme a fuckin' break! Likewise, some lesbians think I am confused, in denial, or suffering from a need to be accepted by men. One even accused me of trying to 'pass' as a straight woman. I told her that I didn't need to fit into one of her boxes and to check herself.

"If we could all just leave the stereotyping alone, we might realize and embrace the continuum within each of us called sexuality. We might learn that a boy or man who can cry and express his feelings isn't being weak or a pussy, he is simply trying to be human. Get it—hu-MAN! He is still a man! The same thing goes for my sisters out there who fear that they can't express all of who they really are deep down inside. I see right through your bullshit."

Request #2: **Start challenging homophobia in settings where lesbians aren't able to, or where we aren't present. We can't always defend ourselves.**

In my work as an organizational-development consultant to corporate America, I have talked with thousands of black professionals about what they expect from their white colleagues and friends. Often, they tell me that they are suspicious of white Americans who claim they are free of bias and racism. When I ask black professionals how they can tell a "trustworthy" white person from other whites in the workplace, they say they look for instances where that white colleague has defended black colleagues in the face of racism. White Americans are often called upon to demonstrate this kind of integrity in situations where black people are not present, or where they would be in danger if they tried to confront racism. This is a great risk to take, since black folks are certainly not totally accepting of white folks, even those who fight racism. White Americans who confront the racism of other whites in circumstances where blacks are not present or able to take up the fight show that they are willing to take the heat to stand in favor of racial equality. That is what it means to be human first.

In social terms, black people who are straight hold a trump card based on the unearned privilege of being straight, which is still very much the societal norm. Unlike the criteria we apply to black/white relationships, we don't hold ourselves similarly accountable to our lesbian, gay, bisexual, or transgender (LGBT) sisters and brothers, who frequently get "trumped" by straight blacks. When I spoke with lesbian and straight sisters together, lesbians talked about the ways in which homophobia denies all black women a deeper experience of sisterhood.

Jill, a Jamaican American lesbian mother with a black American partner, described how she was treated by the black women she worked with as a sales representative for a large telecommunications company in the South. "There are single moms out there in the workplace who meet people like me and they become our friends. But when it comes to their parenting role, especially of their boys, they let their LGBT friends and colleagues down. It's part of the baby's daddy drama. You see, the baby's daddy, who lives elsewhere with the second, third, or fourth wife, mistress or girlfriend, tells his son that it is macho to disrespect women. Then the son comes to Mommy with questions about people who look gay, lesbian, or transgendered, and mommy just totally blows their questions off. This sends the message to the son that something is wrong with you if you are gay and lesbian. Yet, at the same time Mommy has friends in the workplace who are gay and lesbian. I just think that moms have to be a little bit more conscious in terms of fostering sisterhood. Also, those same single moms will say things behind my back when guys in the office make comments about my sexual orientation. For example, they will laugh along when they hear the guys in the office joking about me, saying that I am a dyke with a child, and how they wouldn't want to be raised by two lesbians. I don't always expect straight black women to stand up and say, 'You shouldn't say that,' because women have it hard enough in corporate America and they are too busy looking out for their own backs. However, I think often it's just a little *too* OK for them to allow these guys to disrespect their lesbian sisters.

"A consequence of this collusion is that my partner and I only have two straight black female friends with children. The rest of our straight female friends with children are white. That really concerns me because I want my son to grow up being exposed to and accepting of all kinds of people—black and white, straight and gay. My two straight black friends who are mothers both promote sisterhood, and they are very open-minded. One of them has a lot of lesbian friends, so my partner and I feel comfortable being around her socially, including as a family with our son. I have never felt like I was the token lesbian or Jamaican friend in either of their lives. Now, while my other friend is very accepting, she still has to deal with her family's homophobia in accepting that her close friend is a lesbian. For example, her children don't know what to make of my relationship with my partner, because my friend doesn't publicly acknowledge us as a couple. It's like, 'don't ask, don't tell'. Now I realize that I am suffering from my own internalized homophobia, since I haven't confronted her about her silence. But for God's sake, I am her daughter's godmother! As a friend for twenty-five years, I do expect to feel a little more validated by her in the presence of her children."

Jill was essentially asking her straight black sisters to step out-side of their comfort zones in an effort to support her full participa-tion in black society. Unearned privileges and "heterosexism" can also hinder platonic love and trust among black women.

Request #3: **Continue checking your heterosexism and unearned privilege because it keeps us from loving and trusting you as sisters.**
Many black women feel as if the cards they have been dealt in America are for the most part stacked against them. It is this very mindset that fuels the myth of strength that continues to bind so many black women. Seldom do black women feel like they possess unearned privileges or advantages; but in relation to les-bian women, many of them do, just because they are straight. Unlike earned privileges, unearned privileges are awarded be-cause of who you are rather than what you have accomplished. In our society, being a white, heterosexual, physically able male (none of which any individual can take personal responsibility for being) assures you of possessing the prize deck that is most disproportionately stacked with trump cards.

If you are a heterosexual black woman, you experience un-earned privileges over your lesbian, bisexual, or transgendered sisters—in ways that may be imperceptible to you. In several interviews I had with black lesbians, they commented on the sometimes subtle, and other times brutal, ways in which straight black women used their privilege trump cards in their interac-tions with black lesbians.

Kelly, a fifty-one-year-old lesbian from the Midwest, expressed frustration with some of her straight black sisters because of the double standard she experiences in her friendships with them: "We still live in a world where I can't marry the person I love because of my gender preference, yet many of my straight girlfriends call upon me for marriage advice. While they will acknowledge that I have a girlfriend, for the most part they don't want to hear about my relationship troubles. They just don't want to go that deep with me. Consequently, they tend to be more shallow friendships be-cause they don't care enough about me to want to know my truth.

The religious black women who have chosen me as a friend under the pretense that they can hate the sin and love the sinner have hurt me the most. They either try to pray me straight, or even worse, they simply will not acknowledge that I am a lesbian. This makes me mad because I acknowledge them and deserve the same love and respect in return.

"Once, when I was attempting to tell a straight girlfriend of mine about a date I had with a younger woman, she responded by telling me, 'Honey, to each her own, but that is T.M.I. for me.' T.M.I. means too much information. Well, I was really upset when she said this to me since I was the shoulder that she had been crying on for the past five months since her husband was laid off from his job.

"I also feel like my life experiences and the wisdom I have gained because I am a lesbian has little or no currency in the lives of some of my straight black sisters. How I raise my children, the decisions I make as a mother, my perspectives about men, all of that seems less significant in their eyes because I am a lesbian."

Checking your unearned privileges as a black person is difficult because many of us spend so much of our time dealing with the consequences of racism. It might seem like an impossible task to be able to identify and manage the unintentional benefits that straight blacks may receive merely because of sexual orientation, but solidarity among all black people will be strengthened by our willingness to do so. Getting your hands and heart around how to check your heterosexism can be a daunting task, so here are some questions to get you thinking about the unearned privileges you may experience as a straight black person.

1. How would you feel if your children had to answer questions about why you live with your partner (your husband or boyfriend)?

2. How would you feel if your children were given schoolwork and textbooks that did not reflect or support your kind of family unit (mother, father, kids)?

3. How would you feel if social pressure turned your kids against your choice of a partner?

4. What would you do if you couldn't travel alone or with your spouse without expecting embarrassment or hostility from the people you encounter?

5. How would you respond if most people you met saw your partner relationship as a liability, or used it to judge your whether you were likeable, or competent, or even mentally healthy?

6. What would you do if you couldn't talk about the social events of your weekend without fearing most listeners' reactions?

7. Where would you go if you couldn't feel welcomed and "normal" in the usual walks of public, institutional and social life?

The examples above were adapted from an article about unearned privilege written by Peggy McIntosh of the Center for Research on Women at Wellesley College. A lot of the examples mentioned above are things that "normal" black people take for granted. Checking unearned privileges means challenging our assumptions about the consequences of many of the things we take for granted as straight black people. It also challenges us to confront ourselves and others to ensure that those same unearned privileges are granted to all black people, regardless of sexual orientation.

Straight Black Sisters' Requests of Their Lesbians Sisters

Request #1: **Stop male-bashing, because it creates a distance that we can't afford to have as sisters.**
Cathy, a forty-year-old, single, straight black woman who lives in Oakland, had the following to say about some of the challenges of maintaining friendship across lines of sexuality: "I have noticed that when a lot of hard-core, closed-minded black lesbians get together, they bash men. I mean they will call a brother a nigger just

as quick as some brothers will call a woman a bitch. First of all, it makes me feel judged because I don't share in their sentiments. Now I have to be fair and say that even straight sisters will dog the brothers, but I don't hang around straight women with that kind of mentality either. That's not cool, and in those situations Ifeel very uncomfortable. I guess in the end, it all comes down to attitude: how do you feel about yourself as a woman? The way I see it, being a lesbian is not about hating men; it's about loving women. I'm not straight because I hate women; I'm straight because I love men—sexually and romantically, that is. But I also love my brothers and sisters, straight and gay, unconditionally. I hate dividing lines. If black women are going to jump this hurdle to sisterhood, we have to be more sensitive to each other's realities. My lesbian friends and I try to find things to do that aren't all straight or all gay, like poetry slams and cultural events. That way we can create a comfort zone that works for everybody. Otherwise, we will remain divided as sisters because of who we choose to love."

In addition to male-bashing, straight black women sometimes get stuck in the middle when embracing friendships with black lesbians. On the one hand, they want to promote sisterhood and acknowledge the bond that exists between all women regardless of sexual orientation, but on the other hand, they are committed to creating healthy, intimate, loving, and supportive relationships with men. In a patriarchal society, it is difficult but not impossible to have it both ways. Many straight women who befriend lesbians find that they must take some heat for their open-mindedness from homophobic black men. They must also endure some heat from black lesbians whose anger and resentment toward men can become so strong that they become male-bashers. The result is tension that creates an emotional distance between straight and lesbian women. Remember, truly loving someone who is different from you in a significant way is still an uncommon act in our society. It is far easier to embrace and endear ourselves to other people when they share our values, opinions, attitudes, likes, dislikes, and lifestyle choices.

Jessica is a twenty-five-year old straight black woman who

resents some of the unfair labeling and rumors that can get started because of her friendships with gays and lesbians: "My brother is gay, and I have always been around gays and lesbians. Many of my close friends who are lesbian are really cool. I don't feel uncomfortable or put upon in any way because our friendship is based on much more than who we kick it with. However, what can sometimes be a challenge is how to do things with my lesbian friends that don't make me uncomfortable because I am the only straight woman in the room. Let me clarify what I just said. I don't have a problem with being the only straight sister at a party with gay men and lesbian women, but I do mind when people make unfair assumptions about me. If I am at a predominantly lesbian party with a lesbian friend, I recognize that some of the women will automatically assume that I might be a lesbian. That's only a natural conclusion to draw. But what really annoys me is when the tacky side of a person comes out. I mean, if I tell you or my friends tell you that I am straight, take it as the truth! I am straight—not in the closet and not bi-curious."

Request #2: **Start building bridges based on our need for sisterhood, because it takes all of us working together to eliminate racism and sexism.**

All of the black women I interviewed agreed that there is a real need to strengthen the bonds of sisterhood among black women in America. When I asked how black women of all sexual orientations can begin to build bridges to greater sisterhood, a number of women offered suggestions. Cheryl, a young, straight, single black female attorney from Atlanta, said that she experiences a real sense of sisterhood from her book club. "My book club is an opportunity for all different kinds of sisters to come together because of our love of books. It's through my book club that I've had a safer space to understand some of the challenges and unique perspectives that black lesbians face. I've been able to examine some of my stereotypes as well. I remember when we read our first E. Lynn Harris book and began to discuss the characters, it occurred to me that there might be someone in the room who was in the closet. Almost immediately after the thought passed through my mind, one of the other members, a very refined and attractive sister from Los Angeles, came out of the closet to the group. She talked about how she could relate to the main character in this book because of the stereotypes she faced as a black lesbian who could 'pass' for straight. I must admit I was shocked. Of all the women in the room, she's the last person I would have assumed was gay.

"Thanks to the book club, it made it a lot easier for another lesbian to eventually come out of the closet. It served as a bridge for all of us, straight and gay, because it brought us together as book lovers while inspiring us to grow as sisters.

Straight and gay black women have a lot in common. As mothers, daughters, sisters, and co-workers, you can help each other by sharing experiences and lessons that enhance your lives. By taking an interest in each other's world, you can identify new ways and perspectives for responding to the challenges and opportunities facing all black women. The strategies that seem to work most effectively are those that enable black women of diverse sexualities to keep an open mind, a clear heart, and an attentive ear to doing everything that can be done to promote sisterhood.

Request #3: Continue to engage us in sister-to-sister dialogue.

Many straight black women I interviewed admitted that they are willing to talk to their lesbian sisters and learn more about their unique struggles and victories, but they don't want to probe or appear nosy. So instead, they only respond to or acknowledge a lesbian friend's sexuality when it is placed on the table for discussion. One straight woman told me, "I don't want my lesbian friends to think that I only see them as lesbians. However, I do realize that I feel less comfortable bringing up issues of an intimate nature or raising questions to lesbians, for fear that I might be saying or asking something in an insensitive manner." This comment is a good example of the walking-on-eggshells feeling that many straight black women experience when a conversation moves to sexuality.

In general, we are a conservative and very private people. Many of us were taught not to "air our dirty laundry" or "tell all of our business," lest it should rise again to "slap us in the face." As a result, we overlook or downplay a lot of what we observe in our lives and in the relationships we have with our sisters and brothers. We avoid using words or phrases that acknowledge a person's sexuality. Even the terms "lover" and "partner" are marked as "homosexual" terms in straight culture. They still carry a stigma with them in many black social circles.

Be that as it may, most of the straight black women I spoke to want black lesbians to engage them as sisters in their lives. They are willing to push the boundaries of their comfort zones and examine their unearned privilege to create a greater space for sisterhood across lines of sexual orientation. Jenna, a straight black woman whom I interviewed, remembers the peculiar but loving relationship between her mother and her Aunt Debra: "For all I know, my mother and Aunt Debra were lesbians. After my father left, my mother did her best to raise us with what she had. Aunt Debra wasn't really our aunt, but she was my mom's closest friend and they did everything together. She was like a second mother to me, and she loved me like a daughter.

"Aunt Debra never married and never seemed to have a gentleman calling or coming around while I was growing up. She gave us lunch money, brought us school clothes when Mom didn't have the money to do it on her own, went to church and Sunday school with us, and joined us for Sunday dinner. I even remember several times while growing up when Mom and Aunt Debra went away on vacation together. I have always wondered about the real deal between her and my mother. What I can say is that they were best friends, joined-at-the-heart kind of friends. They gave each other a lot of joy, laughter, and support for as long as they both lived. If Aunt Debra hadn't been a part of my mother's life, I might not be the person I am today, and my mother would have missed out on a lot of love and attention that she wasn't getting from anybody else. Maybe they were just friends. At this point I will never know. What mattered most is that they were like sisters to each other."

Several of the black women who participated in the focus groups and interviews I conducted for this book said that they had never had the opportunity to talk so openly and honestly about creating sisterhood across lines of sexual orientation. However, after each focus group, everyone who participated said that the conversation revealed inaccuracies and fears that drove their assumptions about people of different sexual orientations. What I learned is that regardless of sexual orientation, all black women still want the same thing at the end of the day: to love and be loved. Creating opportunities to love ourselves, with all of our complexities, can only ensure that we will create greater bonds of love with others.

Sisterhood is only one form of love, a platonic love that can help black women heal and laugh and love more fully and completely than they can imagine. Reach out to those in your life who are different but still deserving of your love and sisterhood, regardless of their sexual orientation or preference.

AFFIRMATION

No matter what,
you're my sister and I love you!

8 DOING THE WORK THAT MATTERS MOST: CREATING MEANINGFUL LIVELIHOOD (SELF)

To be who you are and become what you are capable of is the only goal worth living. ALVIN AILEY

ONE OF THE MOST VALUABLE LESSONS I EVER LEARNED ABOUT creating meaningful livelihood came when, as an idealistic and very naive professional, I was hired into a senior executive position at a Fortune 100 corporation. Upon my arrival I decided to try to meet with one of the company's most senior minority executives, an African American woman who was one of the most senior-level leaders of this multibillion-dollar international corporation. I hoped to gain some insight about how to best navigate the landscape of this new corporate culture and ascend the corporate ladder.

My new role in this organization was to engage the leadership and the rest of the company in an ongoing process of culture change. I was hired to help create a workplace environment that celebrated and leveraged the diversity that existed among its employee population. That diversity was vast, so my tasks included helping leaders of the company to address everything from sexism, racism, and other forms of discrimination, to promoting teamwork, creativity, and new ways of thinking. I was excited to meet with this executive because she had received a lot of positive recognition in the black professional community as a groundbreaking woman who had risen to the top of a white-male-dominated corporation. I wanted to know how she had done it. How did she make it to the top? How did she beat the odds? What was she doing to bring others along who looked like her?

When we met, and I began to talk about the challenges before me, she was less than optimistic about my likelihood for success at changing the culture of this same organization that had been the catalyst for her professional achievements. "Listen, you are not going to change the world here," she said, as I enthusiastically shared my vision for my newly created position. I responded, "But the world can change one person at a time. Look at the contribution you have made to this organization." Looking withdrawn, she looked at me and said, "I am only here to do what I was hired to do."

I walked away from that meeting dazed. This was totally out of character with every article and interview I had read about this woman in the pages of Black America's most respected publications. She didn't sound or behave like the fearless, confident, inspiring, visionary leader that all of her press clips represented her to be. Instead, she seemed almost lifeless, going through the motions, and most of all not doing anything to support the kind of challenging yet positive change that I was calling upon her to help me with as a senior leader in this organization. I thought to myself, she is filled with as much hopelessness as many of the black professionals I have met at lower levels in corporate America.

Over the next year, I watched her from a distance. I talked to colleagues who had worked with her. They remarked that she could not mentor other black professionals for fear of being seen as giving preferential treatment. Meanwhile, the word of the day at that time was mentorship. White leaders were mentoring their own in formal and informal settings, but for this lone black female executive, the same practice bore severe consequences.

A year after our conversation, I was invited to a reception at her home, a fabulous minimansion in a posh multicultural neighborhood. She and her husband were "on" that night: she seemed more like the person I had read about, a vital and invigorating take-no-prisoners black female corporate amazon. Toward the end of the evening, after everyone had consumed a few too many of the top shelf martinis being served, I managed to have a brief chat with her husband. I remember this conversation clearly because it shed a great light on the space between the facts and fiction of her life in corporate America.

"How does she do it?" I asked. He responded that as a couple they had decided that since her career was taking off, he would be there to support her. So they made all of the decisions necessary to place her and her career advancement on the best possible path for success. It wasn't until I asked him if his wife was happy with the sacrifices that she had made for her career that I got some insight into why this woman wore so many different masks. He told me that his wife worked long days under intense stress, and that concerned him. He noticed a few years earlier that his wife had developed a new habit. Upon returning home from work each day, she entered the house and before she would do or say anything, she ran upstairs, took off her clothes, and took a long, hot, shower. After thirty minutes, she would appear in the kitchen able to be her regular self again.

This ritual intrigued me. Was it her way of washing away the residue of a spiritually unfulfilling work life? Her husband said that he had learned not to even ask her what she wanted for dinner before she had a chance to take her shower.

I saw that for her, taking a shower after work each day was a profound act of reclaiming that part of herself—the inner part of herself—that she suppressed and sacrificed as part of making it in the workplace. Do you know black women in the workplace whose personal energy and attitude shifts significantly as a result of the roles they feel they have to play in order to survive? Some will tell you their sacrifices are worth it; others say they feel trapped, but too invested to walk away from it all. However, more and more Strong Black Women are creating new ways of working that are in greater alignment with their soul's purpose on this planet.

Creating meaningful livelihood is about doing the work that nourishes your soul, while at the same time feeding your body and paying your bills. Fattening your pocketbook is the path to comfort, not inner contentment. More black women are being called upon or choosing to create work lives that fulfill the deeper need of their souls to make a contribution through work that lifts their human spirit in some way.

Some women arrive at this decision after they have retired,

others after they have been laid off, while some make the decision to create meaningful livelihood at the very beginning of their careers. No matter the course your life has followed, doing the work that matters most in your life is one of the most empowering acts of love, self-care, and joy a Strong Black Woman can give herself. It is a tough choice to make, to trade in your good-paying job for a good-feeling job. But in life, what you give up isn't as important as what you go after. Are you going after more love, self-care, and joy in your work life?

The four stories in this chapter talk about women who, for very different reasons, decided to do the work that mattered most in their lives. There are lessons and wonderful words of wisdom in their stories. As you read them, think about what more you can do to pursue the work that matters most in your life.

The Women of LIFFT

AS THE LEADER OF LOW INCOME FAMILIES FIGHTING TOGETHER (LIFFT), Jeraline Boarders is a love-charged rocket who begins every meeting with prayer. As a matter of fact, each member of this organization is called a "Rocket." Boarders, who is known, loved, and respected as "Ms. G." (as she explained, "When I came to this organization everyone thought my name was Geraldine, not Jeraline, so the organization named me Ms. G. Now, everyone around the world that knows of me calls me Ms. G."), is the first leader of LIFFT, the organization she founded in 2000 through the Miami Workers Center (www.MiamiWorkersCenter.org). I met her, along with Mary Nesbitt, another leading love-charged rocket, and other members of the organization, at their modest but warm storefront office headquarters in Miami.

The Miami Workers Center is a strategy and organizing center for low-income communities and low-wage workers in Miami-Dade County. Started in March 1999, the center's mission is to work to end poverty and oppression. They do this by building the power of grassroots organizations made up of and led by the people most affected by these problems, and by assisting in the development of a broad-based social justice movement in South

Florida. LIFFT is the center's first grassroots initiative and it's rapidly becoming one of Miami's most dynamic organizations; the organization works for fundamental changes in Miami's low- and no-wage economy by battling for state support through grassroots organizing and political education.

Meeting the leaders of LIFFT was one of the most memorable experiences I've had. Through their survival experiences and their love for those who are disenfranchised and voiceless, each of them truly represents what it means to be Strong, Black, and a Woman. In the last four years they have waged a David-versus-Goliath fight centered on affordable housing and income supports such as child care and transportation for welfare recipients and low-wage workers. Most recently they are fighting exclusionary gentrification, increasing access to and employment in child care, and demanding accountability for privatized public services like welfare.

The story of the Miami Workers Center and LIFFT cannot be separated from the story of Ms. G.'s life. It was the logical next step for a Strong Black Woman who woke up one morning from another lonely night in Miami's predominantly black low-income neighborhood, strangely enough called "Liberty City." One day, as she tells it, not unlike so many others, divine providence called upon her and she said, "Enough is enough." Freeing herself from a life of substandard day wages and chronic alcoholism, Ms. G. made a series of life decisions that changed the course of her life from cleaning rich white people's homes on Miami Beach to fighting to save poor black people's homes in Liberty City. Miami, statistically the poorest large city in America as of mid-2004, owes her a great heaping thank you. Her work, and that of everyone else at the Miami Workers Center, has positively touched the lives of people in the one community that most Miamians are trying to forget about.

"When I came to The Miami Workers Center I was upset because a program called Hope Six, from the U.S. Department of Housing and Urban Development (HUD) was trying to take over the low-income projects. Hope Six was a destructive machine that was trying to stop and reduce low-income housing here in Miami and all around the country. Hope Six came to Miami in 1999. They bought the low-income project James C. Scott right out from under the tenants' noses. I lived at James C. Scott Project a couple of years when I was married. Now I live in the Liberty Square projects. I've grown up here in Miami since I was eight years old. I raised six children here and they're all grown now. And I'm still in this low-income project. I've worked two jobs, had a husband, and still was never able to get out of the low-income housing. I look at it as this is where God placed me to be because I've never had a higher income to allow me to me get out of the projects. I worked on Miami Beach as a housekeeper five days a week for thirty years. I got married and pregnant at fifteen years old. This was my life until the new millennium came.

"In 2000, I was an alcoholic. I became tired of the life that I was living as an alcoholic. I thought of bettering my life by going back to school and bettering my education. My mind said, you have nobody to go home to, because I am a widow. So every night I would come home from work and take a bath, and I would get ready to go to school. One night while standing at the bus stop, I saw a lot of people gathered at the community building. I learned that they were talking about the fact that the government was thinking about tearing down Liberty Square Project, where I live. A week later, a young man came to visit me at my house and asked to speak to me about an organization that he was involved with. It was composed of a group of women who were fighting against unfair wages. The group was called Minority Families Fighting Against Wages. I joined the group. This man was an organizer with the Miami Workers Center. I was in that group a couple of months and we had a few meetings and I liked it. So I stayed in the group, but I could only attend on Friday since I went to school Monday through Thursday. We used to meet at each other's house. We had no money and we had no office....so eventually that group broke up. When that group broke up, I stayed with the folks at the Miami Workers Center. I traveled with them to other cities to provide support to other low-income causes like the farm workers. We were working with the farm workers on a two-day march to fight against low wages because the tomato pickers were asking for a penny increase from Taco Bell.

"Another woman from the disbanded group stayed with me and we started recruiting new members. In 2001, we renamed the organization LIFFT. I was the first leader of LIFFT. I was the first person that Tony Ramada from Miami Workers Center organized. After we formed, we got a lady named Ms. Erie Mae Bendross. As membership grows, people go from being members on up to leaders, from leaders on up to the planning committee, and from planning committee to organized leader. Today I am the organized leader. The late Ms. Bendross and I were the first two rockets, the leaders of LIFFT. Now Ms. Mary Nesbitt and I, as well as others, are moving LIFFT forward.

"All of the low-income projects in Liberty City and all around Miami-Dade County are being boarded up. They will not fix them and move people in, when there are thousands of people on the waiting list in urgent need of homes. Last year there were 1,300 boarded-up houses. This year there are 1,700 boarded-up houses. Why aren't those buildings being repaired and offered to people who need homes? This is as much about class as it is about race. Rich people against poor people, rich black people against poor black people, and white people against black people. That is what we must fight against in our struggle to create homes for people who need and deserve them.

"Last year we put on the pressure to the City of Miami. We made a plan to upset the office of the top government official who was responsible for what was happening in our community. We wanted to have a discussion and we walked in the rain to talk to him. We took sixty-five people—adults and children—with pillows and blankets. I told the official that we weren't leaving until we spoke to him. We spoke and set up a taskforce to present a proposal on how to fill the vacancies. I explained to them that the county loses money when they board up the empty units. People break into them, it causes crime, and it costs money, because the county has to deal with that.

"After meeting with the official, we were able to rally enough public attention and support that we got one woman and her six children who had been kicked out onto the streets back into a furnished home in North Miami. They even got costumes and Halloween candy for her kids. Initially, they wanted to send her to an alternate home site that was over ninety minutes, one way, by car from her job. And she don't have no car. So they found what is called a 'scattered-site' three-bedroom townhouse near her job. Now I know they are beginning to listen. So next we took all the people who we knew and who were on the waiting list and we had them send letters to the government official's office so he would not forget how great the need is for low-income housing. We are meeting with him and his team to continue to find homes for those low-income citizens who need them."

Ms. G. had the following to say to Strong Black Women who live in the 'hood: "For the black woman that lives in the 'hood, you can't stay in that box in the 'hood. You've got to come out of the box. This is what I have instilled in my children. Just because you were raised up in the projects, that doesn't mean that you are going nowhere. You can come from anywhere, but it is where you are going that counts!"

Mary Nesbitt offered the following thoughts on self-care: "It is not easy taking care of yourself when you have to fight for all the little things: food, clothing, shelter, and respect. But I don't believe in sitting at home and having a pity party with my arthritis, feeling sorry for myself because my eyesight is going. You know the people who complain because they didn't have any shoes to wear? Well, they went down the street, there was a man that didn't have any feet. So you may not have a pair of shoes, but at least you have your feet."

Her faith keeps Ms. G. going: "If you are ever in doubt, go to your religion. Talking to God every day will help you solve anything, any worry. I used to have all kinds of worries, drinking and everything that goes with it. But, talking to God has made me want to do something with my life and make something of myself. Talking to God has enabled me to become a leader. Soap operas, playing cards, and drinking alcohol was my life before LIFFT. I have been watching soap operas since 1959, when I was pregnant with my first child. Now I just tape them and watch them when I come home after a full day at LIFFT. Now they are for relaxation, not escape. LIFFT is my life. LIFFT has taught me to never give up. You can give out, you can get tired, but through faith, you will never give up."

Helping the World to Feel the Vibe

THE VISUAL POLITICS OF RACE AND GENDER IN THE UNITED STATES of America is evident anytime we turn on the television, flip through a magazine, watch a movie, or just go out for a walk. If you are a black person, it gets personal. First is the sense of invisibility—not being seen or regarded as a vital, contributing member of the society that you live in. Second is the narrowing of our breadth and misrepresentation of our truth, which is expressed by the over-accentuation of the negative versus the positive realities of being black in daily American life. Third is the fear—the clutching of the handbags, the tight grasp of a young white child's hand by her parent when they encounter a black person in the course of daily life. All of this and much more is a result of the conditioned negative vibe towards most things black that our society has inculcated in all Americans—whether black, white, or other—as participants in a social power hierarchy of race- and gender-based privilege and identity. In this country we like happy endings and pretty pictures. Black people live in an America today where happy endings and pretty pictures almost uniformly reflect images of whiteness.

So how do black Americans nurture the richness of our own identity? How do we take care of ourselves in a world of distorted and demeaning visual denigrations of the black aesthetic? How do we celebrate the diversity of our lives, our looks, and our authentic self-expression under a larger social schema that promotes sameness? For Rosie Gordon Wallace, founder and curator of Diaspora Vibe Gallery in Miami's tony Design District (www.DiasporaVibe.com), the answer to these questions was to support and celebrate the creation of art from the Caribbean and African American diaspora that speaks to, validates, and shares with the world who and what we are.

"Unequivocally, I am doing the work that is most meaning-ful to me," said Rosie. "Very few black women realize what their many gifts and talents can bring into their lives. For me, the gifts I have of loving people and of nurturing are integral to my doing what I am doing. Diaspora Vibe is a gallery and incubator space that documents the artistic acts of will and memory of members of the African diaspora. It is my desire to document a generation of young artists who I am going to call the first educated gen-eration in America of immigrants from the Caribbean and the Americas. I want to harness the energy and resources that will enable them to document and work through their visual work. The gallery's passion is to foster the creation of art in all of its forms, but not crafts. Mixed in the message of what I am doing is the effort to dispel the misperception most North Americans have that artistic work from the African diaspora has to be work of craft, and that diaspora work is not contemporary work. The loose definition of contemporary work is that produced by artists who are documenting the work of the now, of the present. Our artists are doing that and they are graduating from meaning-ful schools around the country. In order to document the work, we have to do the work. We have to organize, promote, nurture, incubate, and provide a space for which artists can feel a sense of ownership, belonging, and validation.

"The Caribbean and African American diaspora represents to me the scattering of people here in North America. People of African descent have settled in meaningful numbers in North America. It is part of the broader African diaspora brought about by slavery. Slavery was the original forced scattering of Africans over the globe into Australia, Europe, the Caribbean, and the Americas. The core of my passion is embodied throughout the Caribbean diaspora, and that fuels my desire to do the work that I am doing.

"My personal 'scattering process' into North America hap-pened early in my life. My birthplace was Kingston, Jamaica. Mine is not a typical immigration story. I came to this country as an emotional escape, to get away from a marriage that had gone south. I came here because I wanted to be in a country where the voice of a woman was validated and protected. As bad as we do here, we are better than anywhere else. I came here in 1979 with a five-year-old, three suitcases, $56, and the promise of a job. I immigrated with a lot of tears, anticipation, and hope; however, I didn't have fear, because I was empowered. I knew that I was going to be able to earn. When you can take care of yourself, it eliminates a lot of fear.

"My formative years were in Jamaica and in England, and my actualizing years happened here in America. This is where I became a woman. My background is medical microbiology with a specialty in immunology. I had skills that I could translate into earnings. When you come from a small place, the need for you to perform at a high level is greater than when you come from a big place. My first job was in infectious diseases with Dr. Thomas Hoffman, who was the first to give me an opportunity and who become my mentor and advocate.

"I started Diaspora Vibe Gallery because a young Jamaican complained to me that he was getting ready to graduate from art college after four years. In all of his preliminary introductions to gallery settings and museums, there was absolutely no interest in his work. No one was excited about the fact that this young black artist had found his chosen profession or that he wanted to become an artist. Nobody thought he would be able to make a living. He began to think that if he had spent the four years doing something else, he would have landed on more fertile ground. I was appalled. As an immigrant you are told that you should get your education, but in the end it is not a guarantee to access or to success. I encouraged him to gather a few of his friends who felt the same way and we would try to do something to ensure that there was support for their talent. We started meeting in my garage at home. We talked about what it means to be an immigrant—the politics, the art, and the culture. Who were we going to collaborate with in the art world to create a space and opportunity for Caribbean art and artists in America? I created a formula that consisted of art, music, and cuisine. I thought that if people learned about the art through the culture and cuisine, they would be more likely to buy the art.

"We started meeting to define what happens to artists who are a part of this diaspora. While many of the young artists were born in the states, even their abstract art had a Caribbean vibe to it. It was coming from their generational memory and their inner hunger for the lush sensibility of their ancestors. There needs to be more scholarship about generational memory in the art of our diaspora. It's that part of each of us that is encoded in our memory. Even though you go to school and study European art, the work that is in your soul is the coded expression of your diaspora. When you give the painter a canvas, what she expresses is what resides in her soul. Her training is merely the tool that she uses to express her innermost coding.

"All meaningful work has high points and low points. The highest point is when I am able to use my years of friendships and connections to empower and validate the lives and art of the young people I work with. April Sinclair, a high school intern nurtured through our gallery, was just accepted by the Fashion Institute of Technology. She is a beautiful, talented, young Strong Black Woman. For me to be able to pick up the phone and reach out to those in power to assist her is the greatest thing I can do to validate her dreams. This is how I build the motherland quilt. We are just starting our quilts. We are patterning in the new world and it is an important thing to do. My deepest joy comes from what happens in the lives of the artists and the young people that I work with.

"The lowest point is my inability to have the power to move some of my projects forward due to the limits of funding and sponsorship. My ability to create ongoing sources of funding determines my success in forming generational roots that are reflective of the rich diversity of the African diaspora. I want to be for Caribbean and African American art, in the world of art, what Alvin Ailey was to the world of dance.

"My work in corporate America was significant in that it represented eighteen invaluable years that helped me to define and realize Diaspora Vibe Gallery. The work ethic, the skills, and the challenge of changing people's attitudes and turning those attitudes into actions, was what I learned from my time in corporate America. Now I do the same thing for African American and Caribbean art and artists. My corporate skills prepared me to deal with the economics and politics of art. Corporate America also taught me how to deal as a black person in a white world. I learned that I am not coming from a place of lack. That has assisted me in standing strong and being able to tell my story. I took my cues from the structure of mainstream white culture and corporate America.

"My wisdom for women who have yet to create meaningful work in their lives is summed up by what bell hooks says in her book *Art on My Mind*. She wrote, 'Without culture, without creative art inspiring to the senses, mankind stumbles in a chasm of despair and pessimism.' What better mandate to have in 2004 than to talk to people who are primarily coming from working-class and underclass households, to say the presence of art in your life is absolutely essential to our collective well-being? Our artists need to know that there will be an audience for their work. That's the only way that they will come to this struggle. We must find new ways to celebrate and preserve our culture and well-being, to make sure that this preservation is generational.

"Second, I would advise Strong Black Women to keep a journal. Document the language of your thoughts. Put them on paper so you can go back to them in the hard times. I still have the journal entries from that first meeting in my garage. It inspires me, it calls to me when I lose my way on this path. The thoughts, words, and feelings that we capture from our past are always there to sustain and nurture us in our journey. Journaling is a way we can live by our truths and fight against our fears."

Finally, Rosie offered the following challenge to Strong Black Women who want to create meaningful livelihood. "Women, know your calling. Embrace the work that will change lives. Have the courage to walk away from the false comfort of an unactualized existence. Muster the grit and tenacity to act on and live through your deepest desires. Share your best self with future generations of the diaspora. Generations to come will see your path and take the necessary footsteps to follow in your honor."

A Passion for Truth-Telling

WE ARE ALL PRODUCTS OF OUR PASTS. WE ARE PRODUCTS OF OUR past beliefs, our past behaviors, our past relationships, and our past responses to what life has placed in our paths. When you add these things together, they form our personal histories. Life is something that we understand in review, but if you are a person of color or a woman in America, major parts of the truth about your history have been suppressed, invalidated, or misrepresented to comply with the comfort zone of the larger American mainstream culture. When this happens, your past gets muddied and your sense of self-love and self-care can become damaged. To be American means to live with the consequences of an American history that is revisionist. Americans of all races, genders, ethnicities, religions, and sexual orientations have been denied the cultural and social truths that honestly and accurately reflect the contributions of, and the atrocities inflicted upon, their foremothers and forefathers. Instead of the truth, we are sold a pretty picture intended to make us forget about the inhumane behaviors (many of which are still in practice today) that keep everybody in power feeling good about being in power.

What do you do when what you are told about the legacy of your people doesn't line up with the truth you feel in your soul? What do you do when your instinct and spirit yearns for something that the larger society tells you is not part of the content and character of your tribe? How do you fake it until you make it in a world where "making it" means that you risk losing yourself?

Well, for Leslie Brown the answer came to her one day in a meeting while she was working as a consultant to nonprofit organizations in New York City. Her answer: tell the untold legacy of people whose truths have been suppressed, maligned, and distorted, so that they can begin to heal individually and collectively. On that day, she began the journey to doing what matters most in her life by forming Untold Legacy Production. The mission of Untold Legacy Production is to educate through film, using the historical, accurate, and untold true stories of people of color in America. At the time I spoke to her, Leslie was just beginning to set up her new company. I'm sure you'll see in her words the passion, anticipation, and fear that is common in people taking those initial baby steps down the less traveled road.

"A key component of my evolution was my parents' influence. My father, the late William Harmon Brown, was an independent businessman. I don't ever recall him working for a corporation. He had his own business. My mother, Dr. Peggy Jones Brown, was a teacher and big on the importance of education. She made sure that both my younger brother Chip and I were in private schools because she was so disillusioned with the public school system. My father's independent spirit and my mother's passion to enrich and educate African American and Latino children have both contributed to who I am today.

"Getting to this moment in my life has truly been a fascinating journey. I didn't start out as a teacher or having my own business. I got married and moved to Chicago, where I entered the corporate world. I got a graduate degree in public health, and decided to focus on health care.

"As a little girl, my parents instilled in me the desire to give back. I have been searching for a way to do that most of my life. I realized I was searching for a way to make a positive impact when I got my MPH and then my MBA. When I was attending the school of public health, there were some issues facing members of the African American community there. I immediately wanted to help, but I was told I should focus on my studies, not on the needs of that community. I was warned that if I didn't focus on school over the needs of this black community, I could 'risk not graduating.' That started me down my road to want to help in a big way. I didn't realize how strong my desire was until I got my MBA and took a business development and strategic planning job for a Fortune 100 health-care corporation. In this role, my job was to figure out new ways to make money for the company. However, my thoughts didn't stop there. I figured that if we were going to be taking money from the community in exchange for services, then we should also be giving back to the community. Ultimately, I began to ask myself, what more can I do?

"I used to tutor kids in math at the local church. While I was in my corporate role for the health-care company, I stumbled upon research that indicated that young black boys had the highest asthma mortality rate. So I wanted to do something about this and decided to reach out to a local hospital, La Rabida Children's Hospital in Chicago. They did a lot of work with African American children suffering from asthma and other chronic illnesses. I called them up and before I knew it, I'd helped them to develop a young-professionals board. This new board helped the hospital with fund-raising and bringing greater attention to the plight of sick children in the community.

"The last five years have led me down the road to doing the work that will make the most impact. I had an opportunity to move from Chicago back to my hometown of New York City. I took another corporate job and volunteered with Big Brothers Big Sisters. Once again I found myself frustrated with the politics of the corporate environment, and the lack of opportunity for high-performing, results-oriented black professionals like myself. I noticed that black professionals were often given lateral opportunities instead of promotional opportunities, while their white colleagues of comparable or lesser qualifications and performance were being mentored, sponsored, and ultimately promoted. In addition, I was beginning to pay attention to a deep restlessness and frustration that was stirring inside of me. It was forcing me to confront the need to change direction, to ask myself, 'What else should I be doing?'

"Divine providence is always working in your life. I've learned that sometimes I work with the forces of the universe and that other times I work against them. This time the universe propelled me into the next phase of my journey when I ended up taking a severance package four years after arriving in New York City. After September 11, 2001, the New York job market tanked. I watched many of my friends suffer along with me through this bad economy. I encountered great resistance while looking for work in post-9/11 New York City. But the funny thing about the universe is that when one door closes, another one opens, as they say. I was presented with some once-in-a-lifetime opportunities, such as to visit Cuba. There are truly differences between my plan and the divine plan for my life. So you just keep on knocking on doors until the right one opens which God has intended. I guess you could call that faith.

"I started volunteering for a nonprofit organization that provides consulting to other nonprofit organizations to help them operate more effectively. Eventually I was offered a part-time position as the leader of one of the consulting divisions of this organization. While in this role, I've learned a lot about nonprofit organizations and developed valuable relationships with people in the city and across the country. You know how sometimes things happen in your life and you don't know what to do with it, but you know that in time, it will be made clear to you? Well, that's how I feel about the current part-time executive job I have. I have been gaining valuable knowledge and establishing new relationships. I just didn't know where this experience was heading.

"Untold Legacy Production was born during a conversation I had in a meeting at work. I was speaking with a gentleman who had left corporate America to start his own nonprofit, a creative entertainment and arts program for African American children. He has also created a for-profit product that he wants to market. I was telling him about my desire to educate people about African American history by trying to set the record straight. During our meeting, one of the participants said 'Why not realize your passion through film? It will have a greater impact.' I said 'Wow...that's it! Combining my passion for history and my passion for film, what a great idea!' It felt right! It was as though the restless voice in me spoke through him to help me recognize what I needed to do next in my life.

"I'm at the very beginning of doing the work that matters most in my life. Making Untold Legacy Production a success is probably going to be one of the most significant challenges before me, but I am up for it. This is a huge undertaking and I want to make a great impact."

Choices and Dreams

STRONG BLACK WOMEN HAVE ALWAYS BEEN COUNTED UPON TO DO the work that needed to be done. They have cared for the family while holding full-time jobs. They have nursed their elders when they could no longer take care of themselves. Their strength has benefited so many people that it is no wonder that from early on they were considered the most important unit of slave labor. But the very same conditioning that empowers the myth of the Strong Black Woman has inhibited them from making choices in their lives to follow their passions and cherish their dreams.

All of the women above came to the realization they needed to change the course of their lives in an attempt to do the work that matters most. However, many enlightened young black women today have figured out their passions early on and are making the choices to pursue them at the beginning of their careers. Such is the case for Megan Kirksey, a twenty-five-year-old African American woman who is studying for her MD and PhD degrees. When she isn't performing extensive research to help find a cure for tuberculosis, she is helping people of color from as far away as South Africa to live healthier and happier lives. She learned this passion for service as a little girl from loving parents who stressed the importance of giving back to those who are less fortunate. "I was fortunate to have a good education and supportive parents who always encouraged me to follow my passion and do my best," said Megan. "I'm making a big sacrifice in my life now as I pursue these advanced degrees. It is a gamble because the future is such an unknown, but I know for sure that I am here to help and to heal. I want to prepare myself to do just that, to the best of my ability."

Four Steps to Meaningful Progress

IT IS NEVER TOO EARLY OR TOO LATE TO CREATE MEANINGFUL LIVELI-hood. But taking the first steps can feel like an impossible task. So here are four steps to follow as you move forward to doing the work that matters most in your life.

Listen to your inner voice. That little voice that lives inside all of us is there for a reason. It is the truest part of our soul speaking to us as we make the decisions that affect the course of our lives. Listen without judgment to your inner voice. It will take you in the direction of your soul's purpose. Be very aware of how you feel and how you react to the work you do, and don't be afraid to make the changes necessary to improve the quality of your worklife.

Treat failure as an invitation to grow. When you fail in work, it doesn't make you a failure. There is usually something that you can do differently that you have not previously considered. Don't overreact, instead take time to silently observe your environment for subtle cues. Then set a new plan for moving forward; don't allow yourself to get stuck in humiliation or fear.

Find a mentor and a sponsor. A mentor is someone who can show you the way to realize your career objectives and goals. Oftentimes they understand the path that you must follow, the skills you must develop or refine, and the knowledge you must acquire to realize your personal or professional goals. That doesn't necessarily mean that a mentor has the power or influence to help make things happen in your career. That is why you also need to identify a sponsor. Sponsors play a vital and distinct role in career development. They go beyond the mentor step to help clear the obstacles or facilitate the opportunities that will allow you to make significant progress toward your career objectives. In short, they have the power to provide you with that once-in-a-lifetime opportunity. Your sponsor operates as your broker, someone who—because of her belief in your skill, competency, or potential—will assume the personal or professional risk to give you the break you need to strut your stuff. Sponsors can introduce you to the right people, position you favorably with an audience that you otherwise might not have access to, and talk up your name as the next or hottest new talent in your field. Black women need more sponsors, especially in corporate America. They need powerful individuals who will hold them up and insist upon their candidacy in situations where women of color are often overlooked or minimized. Identify someone who has already been down the road you are traveling and ask her/him to mentor you through your journey. But also, try to cultivate a relationship with a sponsor who will help clear the obstacles and create the kinds of critical opportunities that are necessary for your talents, gifts, and professional goals to flourish. Now remember, when you get down the road a bit yourself, turn around and reach back to mentor and sponsor those precious diamonds behind you.

Don't waste time. Too many people live in the town called "Wouldashouldacouldaville." The easiest way to miss the divine plan for your life is to waste time with delays and excuses about why you can't do something, instead of asking how you *can* do something with your life. Have faith and use your strength in defense of your passion. Each week set a goal and create a task list. Determine the amount of time you will need to complete the tasks that are essential to doing the work that matters most in your life. Identify the emotional and time traps that often stop you from completing those tasks and create new behaviors and strategies to overstep those traps in the future. And most importantly, don't waste time focusing on the mistakes or lost opportunities of the past. Regroup, reclaim, and move forward!

AFFIRMATION

Today I will nourish within myself
the passion to do what I was meant to do,
to give what I was born to give, and
to become all that I have dreamed of being.

9 KEEPING THE FAITH: SPIRITUALITY AS THE SOURCE OF OUR STRENGTH (SELF)

The substance of things hoped for the evidence of things not seen. HEBREWS 11:1

I LEARNED THE IMPORTANCE OF RELIGION FROM THE BLACK women and men in my life. We grew up in a God-fearing family. My parents were pioneering members of the integrated church in my hometown. They were members of the local chapters of the Order of the Eastern Star and the Prince Hall Masons. My brothers and I had to learn a Bible verse and recite it at dinner. We went to church and to Sunday school, we participated in the Methodist youth programs in our community, and we read the Bible each week. When someone died, I was taught that they went to better place if they had taken Jesus as their savior. Many times as a child, when I was expected to accept something that didn't make logical or tangible sense to me, I was told to "just have faith that everything is going to be all right."

Having faith is something that black people have been taught by our elders to cultivate as both a mechanism of religion and survival. Having faith in my life has meant that I am able to somehow find the strength to push forward beyond my point of emotional, physical, or spiritual exhaustion. Having faith in my life has meant that I am able to endure the hurts and attacks of enemies and never let them see me sweat, because I know that in the end God's will prevails. More importantly, it has enabled me to forgive my enemies. Having faith in my life has meant that no matter what happens to me or my loved ones, I have a responsibility to carry on and do what I was placed on this planet to do, even if I don't always agree or understand.

Faith is not about answers or questions, and it certainly isn't about proof or facts. Most people of great faith don't have the answers to questions about how they are going to do what they need to do, except to say that their faith will get them through. As a result, they also don't require answers to explain life's great tragedies or good fortunes. Knowing why something did or didn't go your way in life doesn't require faith. Faith is only cultivated in the dark face of the unknown or uncontrollable. It is the rock upon which we stand, the lighthouse that shows us the safe harbor, and the inner voice that guides us in our decisions. Without it, most Strong Black Women (and men) will tell you that they would be lost.

So what does faith mean in the lives of black people today? Well, the poster child for faith in our society is the Strong Black Woman. When Charisse Jones and Kumea Shorter-Gooden, the authors of *Shifting: The Double Lives of Black Women in America,* asked the black women they interviewed, "What helps you to get through difficult times?" a full 75 percent of the women whom they surveyed volunteered "faith," "God," or "my church." Jones and Shorter-Gooden also referred to a study (The National Survey of Black Americans) that indicated more than 71 percent of black women attend services several times a month; 68 percent of black women are members of a particular church. Additionally, the survey revealed that the religiosity of black people was about far more than going to church on Sunday morning. It also found that prayer was employed as a key strategy by men and women to cope with stressful episodes in their lives.

I don't know about you, but I find great comfort in knowing that I have parents who love me enough to pray for my safety, success, and well being. My mother used to pray when I would travel on business trips. I once had a very religious flight attendant tell me that she prayed for God to place an angel on each wing of every plane she flew on. She said, "I pray from the moment I get on this plane to the moment I get off, and then I praise God for keeping me safe through another flight." Her love for her

God is real and she calls upon it every day through prayer. In the lives of many Strong Black Women, prayer is an essential daily tool of endurance. Faith and prayer restore their souls in times of trouble. It brings them peace in the midst of their storm. It helps them to choose their soul's path when life presents them with a fork in the road. Many Strong Black Women will tell you that you can't cultivate love, self-care, and joy in your life without a deep and abiding faith in God.

What Is Faith Made Of?

BLACK WOMAN PRACTICE MANY DIFFERENT RELIGIONS. I INTERVIEWED black women who practice Christianity, Buddhism, Hinduism, Santeria, and vodoun. I interviewed women who were pastors of their own churches, and I interviewed women who haven't set foot in a church in thirty years, but they all told me they have faith. Furthermore, they all claimed to be women who rely on their faith in some form or another to get through daily life. While religion is certainly a conduit to the establishment of faith in the lives of many Strong Black Women, every woman who goes to church and believes in God is not necessarily a person of deep and abiding faith. Is it possible that faith is something in addition to the rituals, practices, and traditions that distinguish one religion from another? So what is the core denominator of faith in the lives of Strong Black Women? From what I can see based on the women and men I have spoken with, the answer is simple: love.

Let's not forget that love is a relationship. As we talked about in chapter one, your love pie is composed of three slices, Self, Platonic, and Romantic. Together, they represent the total experience of love in your life. But the crust of your pie—the universal and unifying dough that keeps your pie together—is what makes your pie a pie. The crust touches all the contents of your pie, thereby enriching and strengthening it in flavor, form, and texture. What is the crust that gives flavor, form, and texture to your love? What are the ingredients that make up your dough? Is it made of known substances like gender, race, age, class, or religion? What if there was a universal ingredient, perhaps less known and observable, but guaranteed to enrich your love relationships? Would you want to add a pinch of it to your crust?

After almost twenty years of helping people of all cultures, classes, races, genders, ages, and religions to create a healthier, more inclusive, and productive work life, I have come to realize that too often we overinvest our trust and faith in the set of human characteristics that give us our identity. We build our sense of community based on our shared human traits, conditions, and ideologies. When we do this, we are much more likely to avoid and exclude people based on our human differences. We don't love or place our faith in people whom we feel the need to avoid or exclude. Making the dough for your love pie's crust exclusively from a finite set of human similarities and differences will limit the richness of your love relationships.

For the most part in American life today, we love our fellow man or woman only if they are black like me, rich like me, cool like me, or Christian like me. Let me remind you that the most segregated day of each week in this country is still Sunday morning. Breaking free of this limiting condition requires making a crust fortified with the inclusive and universal ingredient called *spirit*. Then, regardless of our human similarities and differences, the spiritual being in me can embrace the spiritual being in you. As spiritual beings we are open to the possibility of love, faith, and trust in every human interaction. Spirit is bigger than you; it encompasses everyone with whom you have a relationship. Whether we acknowledge it or not, it is already an ingredient in everybody's pie crust.

Spirit is that certain something about every human being regardless of race, creed, or color that is real, yet not always known or tangible. We experience it in our relationships as "chemistry" or "vibe"; others call it just a good or bad feeling. Whatever you call it, we all experience a connection with our fellow human beings whether we are meeting them for the first or the hundredth time. It happens before we have time to collect enough data to form an opinion or make a judgment. For those who acknowledge it, spirit is a portal to the nurturing of abundant love, faith, and joy in your life.

Let me give you a brief example of what I am talking about. Pull out your cell phone and scroll through your address book. For most of us, the people who are stored in our cell-phone directories represent people with whom we have co-created significant relationships. Now as you scroll through your cell phone directory, think about how many similarities you share with the people on the list. Are they the same race, generation, religion, gender, socioeconomic status, sexual orientation, or political affiliation as you? Where are the people in your life who don't fall into the same broad categories of humanness as you do? What is the quality of your love relationships with the people listed in your cell phone, and how is it different from those who live outside the broad and comfortable categories of sameness in your life? What if you could create a category that everybody, regardless of their human differences, could be an equal part of? How would your love relationships change if you could define, embrace, and love from that newly formed category of humanity and relationships? How many more entries would you need to add to your cell phone directory to accommodate this new list?

Trust and faith are siblings. It is difficult to cultivate faith without trust, and trust cannot be sustained without faith. Black women have told me that they struggle with the notion of trust. Historically, black women have trusted many different groups of people and been let down. The collective consciousness of black men, white men, and white women has repeatedly violated the collective voice, faith, and reality of black women. Consequently, black women have learned to place their faith in something that is greater than the categories of sameness and difference that shape their individual and group identities. Black women have taken the rap for being strong and angry long enough. It is time to give them a break and to better understand what is really going on when society mislabels, stereotypes, and dismisses black women as angry. What others have mislabeled and stereotyped as black woman's anger is, at the core, her loss of faith in the possibility of engaging a deeper love from her nation and her people. Black women down through the ages have cultivated a strength that has been sustained by love. What others call her attitude of anger is really the Strong Black Woman's recognition that she is not being seen or treated as worthy of voice, identity, and inclusion. What America doesn't see are the tears of the Strong Black Women.

Love or Fear

IN EVERY RELATIONSHIP WE CAN ONLY RESPOND WITH LOVE OR FEAR. Love is empowering while fear is debilitating. A Strong Black Woman's loving response to life calls forth her capacity to impart a deep and abiding faith in all of her love relationships. When she chooses a fearful response to life, this indicates that she feels hurt, disempowered, or unable to respond to life from a loving place. When we become angry, we squelch our capacity to connect in our relationships. Without this connection, we cannot transcend fear, because we have turned away from the source of personal power that is greater than the object of our fear.

Have you ever noticed how catastrophic tragedies enable us for a brief moment to reach beyond our comfort zones of sameness? Have you ever noticed how an unfortunate occurrence beyond anyone's control or blame can prompt the humanity in you to affirm and assist the humanity in others? Our connectedness on this level transcends religion, race, gender, age, language, nationality, and class; it is always available to us, not just when we are called into crisis. This connectedness is our humanity. The sooner we consistently embrace the humanity of the world as black women and black men, the better off we will be. Through the power of our faith, we can show the world the way ahead.

To do so requires individual and collective ongoing acts of black faith. As faith-filled as we are, we could still benefit from cultivating more faith and trust in our fellow man and woman. While we may not change the minds of those who will still interact with us from a place of fear, we can work to create the possibility of transcendent love in the minds and hearts of those people in our lives who want to co-create with us the highest quality of love relationships, be they self-love, platonic love, or romantic love.

The women whose stories I have chosen to share with you live each day of their lives by faith. Their stories are a testament to strength as currency in their lives. But if that currency were a two-sided coin, heads would be the strength that they use to make it in a world that is polarized by love and fear, and tails would be the faith that orders their steps.

No Crystal Staircase

SPUNKY, VIBRANT, AND FULL OF JOY ARE THE WORDS THAT BEST describe eighty-nine-year-old Gertrude Bronson, from Percy, Mississippi. In addition to being a Strong Black Woman, she is someone who embodies deep faith and abundant joy in her life. Her faith grew as a result of her deep love for her father, her sister, and most importantly, her deep love and respect for God.

"Looking back over my life, the main lesson about faith that was established in my life was from my father," she said. "I was born in 1915, on a farm just outside of Percy. When I was six years old, my father first took me out to the field to help him farm our land. I hated farm chores. I realized quickly that I couldn't handle the heat. One day when I was about eight or nine, he was talking to us and he told me, 'If you don't conduct yourself properly, I am going to send you to work on the farm.' From that day I was determined to get an education, because I didn't want to work on the farm.

"In those days, you had a choice of three desk jobs. You could be a minister, a teacher, or a lawyer. If you didn't get one of those jobs, Daddy said you would end up working in 'Mrs. Nutlow's kitchen.' In Mrs. Nutlow's kitchen you had to wash the clothes in a pot in the yard and do the ironing too. I realized that I couldn't do something like that for a livin' because I was not going to make it over a hot pot, and I was not going to make it in the field, so I decided to get my education and get out of Percy.

"Over the years, I never lost my faith, I never wavered from it, not even once. I had to put myself through school because Daddy passed away when I was thirteen. I don't remember my mother because she passed away when I was five, but I always knew she was around me. I could feel her spirit that way. My younger sister and I were raised by my older sister. We didn't know how we were going to eat right after Daddy died, but my older sister Leola became like my mother. She kept us all together, raised us, and kept hold of our father's land in Mississippi. Daddy had an insurance policy that helped us survive after he passed, but we were three young girls and all we had was our faith in each other and what our father had taught us. Leola told us that Mommy and Daddy appeared at the foot of her bed one night shortly after he passed over and told her to make sure that we girls stayed together. So she took care us all of us until we were able to go to college and begin our own lives.

"In college, I cleaned a white woman's house for room and board. During the school year, I worked in the cafeteria. It took a lot of strength to get through life during those days. I never lost my faith or my drive. I always knew that I was meant to leave the South and do better with my life. I ended up taking a job as the first director of nutrition in St. Thomas, Virgin Islands. As a young single woman, I had to shoulder a lot of responsibility and the doubt of a lot of people who didn't think I could do it. But I was strong, I had faith, and I did. When I returned, several years later, I met and married my husband.

"I guess there have been two big tests of my faith in life. One was the death of my husband. But clearly the most challenging test of my faith was the murder of my son. He was my only child, and he was senselessly robbed and murdered by three people when he was twenty-nine. I was devastated, and knew that since I had to forgive the people who killed him, I could not ever go to the courtroom to see their faces. So I didn't go because I knew that I would need to find the strength to forgive them. If I never saw them, it would be easier for me to forgive them.

"The loss of a child will shake your world like no other loss. It makes you re-examine the very meaning of life, but in the end you know that it is God's plan and you learn to accept it. I am lucky because while I lost my son many years ago, I have replaced him with another family relative who has been like a son to me. God is good, he has watched out for me in my old years and gives me the love of the son that I lost many years ago. I didn't know how God would take care of me, but I never doubted that he would.

"Today, I make it through each day by prayer. I don't just pray in the morning when I get up and again at night. I pray all day. It is like I am in constant communication with God and he is in constant communication with me. If people stayed in prayer every day as long as they stay on their cell phones, the world would be a better place. I know that I don't have much more time on this earth, but I don't worry because I have a personal relationship with God that is real in my life. I also know that I am real in His life. Many of us haven't worked on building a personal relationship with God. It is like any other relationship: if it is gonna be a good one, you gotta work at it. Through my relationship with God, I find strength and laughter. I don't dwell on evil. That is a waste of my time and energy. I just dwell on the Lord. He is my friend.

"My faith gives me determination. I never feared much in life, even when my husband's family took all his money after he died. I was hurt, but I didn't have fear. God provided a way. I had my own money, so I wasn't going to be left out in the cold. My faith has always led me to the light when my life seemed like it was in the dark. I have always had the path shown to me. But I had to be willing to walk the path God put in front of me. It didn't always appear when I wanted it to, and it didn't always take me where I thought I should go. But in the end, by talking to God, I knew the road he intended for me to go. Now my life is filled with laughter. I am at peace and I have joy. My faith is what got me through."

A Force for Hope

TALKING TO BISHOP ERNESTINE REEMS IS A LIKE SIPPING A FROTHY mug of hot chocolate on a cold winter's day. She gives you the feeling that everything is all right in the world, because after talking to her you feel good and warm inside. Bishop Reems has the ability to put you at ease and call you to attention all in one sentence. She started our interview by saying, "Now Toby,

I am not going tell you anything that I know your mama hasn't told you."

For the past thirty-five years, Bishop Reems has been ministering in Oakland, California. She established her first church on the corner of 98th and MacArthur at a time when women were still not welcomed in the pulpit. Today she is the minister of Center of Hope Community Church in Oakland, a leader, a mother, a wife, an author, and a woman whose love and faith is the source of her strength.

"We were made to be strong women," she told me. "To combat oppression, we had to create systems of determination, courage, boldness, and faith. My father was a minister, my brother is a minister, and my aunt is a minister, but I had to pay a big price to become one. I had to find my own church and endure different levels of suffering because I am a woman. Thirty-five years ago they didn't believe in women as pastors in my denomination. I kept a husband for forty-two years until he passed away. After he passed, I had to cry, wipe away the tears, and keep pushing, while respecting men. Strong Black Women respect men. I am a praying woman, a respectful woman, and a woman who respects the system.

"I try to tell women that you don't have to go out there and misuse the gifts of femininity that God has given you. Instead, you have to work. If it is served to you on a platter, it is not good for you. Go get your own platter and put what you want on it. I made it this far because I walk in faith. By walking in faith, I walk in obedience to the word of God."

Bishop Reems has not walked alone. Through her strength and faith she has brought a lot of people along on her faith walk. She has started a $6 million housing project for seniors, a $10 million housing project for low-income people, and a faith-based school for 400 students in Oakland. California. And she kept right on walking to South Africa, where she has contributed to similar community development projects.

"Faith is simple. I am gonna walk out the door and while I see nothing, I believe that God is gonna place something there. Faith can only happen when you don't see anything. It happens in the same space that strength is created. Faith is what I hold onto in the midst of adversity. God doesn't honor pity and sadness, but he does honor faith!"

Sustaining the Faith of a Mustard Seed

MS. BRONSON AND BISHOP REEMS ARE TWO WOMEN WHO HAVE walked the planet long enough to discover the source of their strength. Walking through life by faith is a process that unfolds for many of us with age and life experience. As I have grown older, my faith in things has narrowed and deepened. When I was younger I had faith in many things, most of which has been shaken or destroyed by the storms and challenges of my life. The beauty of age is it teaches you to distinguish the solid from the vapor in life. In his book *Stages of Faith,* James W. Fowler has the following to say about the multidimensional character of faith: "Faith is a person's way of leaning into and making sense of life. Faith is the dynamic system of images, values, and commitments that guides one's life."

When I was a little boy, my mother used to tell me, "Dad and I love you so much that if there was an award for the luckiest boy in the world, you would win it hands down." They also told me that their love was so deep that if I was about to be run over by a car, they would jump in front of the car to exchange their lives for mine. Those two statements created a deep and abiding knowledge in me about the power and importance of love. Through their words I always knew that I was deeply loved by at least two people in this world. From that day, my faith in the power of love was born.

Faith gives us a reason to get up in the morning. It gives us a guiding principle to order our lives. It reminds us that the potential that lies within each of us is real, but we have to play to win. It also reminds us that only love is real. By waking up each day to the possibility of cultivating love in your life, you step into your armor of faith.

There is no one way to embrace your faith. It will be easier for some than others. But here are a few questions that James W. Fowler used to get himself in closer proximity to understanding and strengthening faith in his life. Try them on for yourself and remember to keep the faith!

1. What commands and receives my best time and energy?

2. What causes, dreams, goals, or institutions am I pouring out my life for?

3. As I live my life, what power or powers do I fear or dread?

4. To what or whom am I committed in life? In death?

5. With whom or what group do I share my most sacred and private hopes for my life and for the lives of those I love?

6. What are those most sacred hopes, those most compelling goals and purposes in my life?

AFFIRMATION

Today I will walk in faith.

10 RECLAIMING JOY:
MAKING PEACE WITH YOUR LIFE
(SELF)

If you cannot find peace within yourself, you
will never find it anywhere else. MARVIN GAYE

I REMEMBER THE FIRST TIME I SAW SOMEONE "GET HAPPY." I WAS
about eight years old and my family went to an old Baptist church
in Maryland. My brother and I were sitting about six pews in
front of my parents, and directly in front of us was a very large
black woman wearing a big, wide hat and carrying a fan. It was
a hot evening service and the church didn't have air conditioning.
We got to the part of the service where people were invited to
stand up and tell the congregation a story from their lives.

The very large woman sitting in front of my brother and me
stood up and started talking to the pastor and members of the
congregation. We didn't really pay attention to what she was saying or doing until all of a sudden she let out a loud scream. "Thank
ya! Thank ya! Thank ya! Lawd, for bringing me joy in my darkest
hour!" Before we knew what was happening, the woman started
jumping up and down, flailing her very ample arms around in
the air while waving her fan as if to chase away imaginary flies.
This continued for what seemed like a lifetime for my brother and
me. The woman continued to jump and dance and spin around.
She continued to shout, "Thank ya Jesus, sweet Jesus, thank ya
Lawd, you bring me joy!" Then, after reaching a point of total
exhaustion, she fell out. Hurling herself backward, she almost
ended up in our laps. Panicked and fearing for our lives, we made
a quick exit out of the pew and ran down the aisle back to where
our parents were sitting (and at this point laughing) behind us.

A few days later, I asked my mother what had happened to the big lady at church the previous Sunday. She looked at me and smiled and said that the lady had just been touched by God and was filled with the joy of the Holy Spirit. My mother's response made no sense to me at the time. But I never forgot that moment, or my mother's explanation of that woman's seemingly inappropriate behavior.

Have you ever been filled with so much joy and happiness that you just couldn't contain yourself? Let's face it, extremely happy or joyous people in our society today sometimes make us nervous. We tend to respond to them as I did to that woman in the church pew many years ago, with fear. We tend to think to ourselves, what's wrong with this person? What have they been taking? What happened to make them so happy? Is it that we don't believe that people can be truly joyous all of the time? Are we afraid to claim joy for ourselves? Why do many of us become even more alarmed if a person's joy is not fleeting? Do we believe that joy and inner peace can be maintained by any black person as a constant state of being? Have some people figured out how to have too much fun in life? What's up with that?

A number of the Strong Black Women I interviewed for this book know exactly what is up with reclaiming joy and inner peace in their lives. Surviving under the myths and stereotypes of Strong Black Womanhood has made some women lose sight of that part of themselves that is home to their joy. I truly began to understand what many of the women I interviewed were referring to when they said that they had reprioritized the order of love in their lives from romantic/platonic/self to self/platonic/romantic. This helped them reclaim the joy in their lives that they had previously sacrificed or lost to influences outside of themselves. Now they could feast upon their own lives, the bitter and the sweet times, with total compassion and total surrender. Getting to this point involved a process of reclamation for these Strong Black Women. For all Strong Black Women, it involves a homecoming journey to your original self and to a daily practice of self-love and self-care.

If life is a banquet, some of the dishes served to Strong Black

Women have been hard to swallow at times. Nonetheless, life as it uniquely unfolds is spiritual nourishment for our souls. When we turn away from the table called life, we turn away from the sustenance that has been prepared for our spiritual development. If we fail to feast on both the bitter and the sweet, we leave our souls unsatisfied. Reaching a true level of satisfaction, or even joy, is a process that for some can only happen over time; for others, it might come in the form of a monumental conversion experience. Either scenario requires an honest and embracing journey back to ourselves.

My Mother's Greatest Lesson

MY MOTHER'S STORY OF RECLAMATION, WHICH I SHARED IN THE FIRST few pages of this book, was a conversion experience that invited her to reclaim her joy and inner peace. A near-death experience of any kind will compel most people to engage life from a whole new set of values and behaviors. My mother's near-death experience confirmed for her that the spirit in all of us brings joy.

However, the change in her attitude, outlook, and behaviors during the final year of her life revealed to me that self-love and self-care is the process through which we delight the spirit to reclaim joy. Through this joy we can create a deeper level of fellowship with everyone in our lives. We can transform all of our relationships by embracing and defending our joy and sharing it with others. This may be the greatest lesson my mother ever gave me.

The changes my mother made during the last year of her life had a profound effect on everyone she touched. However, we don't all have to wait for life to come along and slap us in the face before we wake up to the possibility of real joy in our lives. We can work each day toward creating and sustaining more inner peace and joy in our lives. You might ask why many men and women never seem to reclaim joy in their lives. For many of us, living as we do in a culture that embraces the "pleasure principle" over the principles of joy, we have lost sight of the difference between joy and pleasure.

Joy Versus Pleasure

LIFE IS FULL OF OPPORTUNITIES TO RECONNECT US TO A DEEPER EX-
perience of love in our lives. The scent from a fresh bouquet of
flowers; the sound of silence at the dinner table that lets you know
that everyone is enjoying the meal you prepared; the warmth of
a pet's playful affection: all of these possess boundless healing
powers. What makes these opportunities more real in the lives of
some women over others is the intention we set about how we engage each moment of our lives. To transform the quality of your
life and reclaim more joy, you must reexamine what brings pleasure and what brings joy in your life. Once you've distinguished
them, you must make a true commitment to reclaim joy in your
own life, and make it a priority above pleasure.

Have you ever met people who seem to have everything money
can buy and still are not happy? Perhaps they have traveled to
the most exotic places in the world, dined in the world's finest
restaurants (without gaining a pound), have the most fabulous
friends, and live in the most spectacular homes, but their lives
are wrought with despair. Why does joy so often elude those who
have access to every pleasure that fortune can buy? Too often,
these people are afflicted by a failure to understand the difference between pleasure and joy, and as a result have been unable
to make the commitment necessary to achieve true joy in their
lives. Unlike pleasure, which is derived through our engagement
with the world we live in, joy is an inner condition. Pleasure is
produced by embracing what is happening in the world around
you, while joy comes from determining your response to the
world based on your self-love and self-care. Joy in action delivers
a peace of mind that drives your peaceful response to every life
circumstance. To be joyful, and therefore make peace with your
life, you must only respond to the circumstances of life in a manner that is well with your soul. You must also stay focused on the
life you are living, not the life you have lived or the life you have
yet to live. Peace of mind and the joy it delivers is something
that we claim in every step throughout our day. We claim peace
of mind in the big decisions of our life like where to live, when

to start a family, or when to buy a home. We also claim peace of mind through the many little decisions of everyday life—smiling at your co-worker in the elevator, or setting aside "me time" to get organized before you begin your day, or allowing yourself time to relax and renew after a challenge-filled day. Staying focused on the present moment of your life is key to sustaining joy.

You may discover that your newfound commitment to reclaim joy in your life might cause conflict in the lives of others, who may have benefited from your previous unwillingness to cultivate more self-care in your life. Jacqui, an African American woman from Chicago, walked away from a very lucrative career as a partner in a law firm to teach English and pursue her creative side. In time, several members of her family dismissed her as crazy. Many of her friends (especially those who were also lawyers) stopped calling after they realized she was no longer available to listen to their complaints about how much they hated their own careers. Within five years, almost everything about her life changed, including her friends and her lifestyle.

"As I look back," she said, "I realize that nobody cared about my unhappiness with my old life more than I did. They actually benefited from it, because I would commiserate with my other lawyer friends when they needed a shoulder to cry on. But once I decided to take control of my life and do what I believed I needed to do to create more peace of mind, some of my friends became very upset with me. Now we wanted different things out of our lives. I wanted to live my best life; they wanted to play it safe."

There is no optimal set of life circumstances that makes one Strong Black Woman better prepared to release herself from the myths, stereotypes, and struggles of her life than another. There is only the burning desire to live your life as a full expression of the love you are *getting and giving*. No other living Strong Black Woman in my life at this time is a greater example of the full expression of love, self-care, and joy than Elinor Jones, fondly known and loved by all as "Miss Ellie." Her life has been full of great highs and lows, victories and defeats. Through it all, she has reclaimed joy for herself and encouraged in the lives she touches a deeper hope, endless laughter, outrageous joy, abiding love, and contentment with self. This is just one woman's story and one woman's wisdom. But as you read it, think about how much love, self-care, and joy you are claiming each day of your life.

How Miss Ellie Got Her Joy Back

ON ALMOST EVERY SUNDAY BETWEEN THE FIRST AND SECOND SERvices at Unity on the Bay church in Miami, Florida, you can find Miss Ellie on the porch of the annex behind the chapel. You will probably hear her laughter and the laughter of many others who take a few moments out of the day to sit down on the porch and chat. As she flashes her million-dollar smile from behind her big, dark Jackie-O sunglasses, she could be talking about anything: one of her stories about traveling the jazz club circuit during the 1950s with her late husband, Count Basie bassist and jazz great Eddie Jones; great lessons she has learned about love and loss from motherhood; scrumptious Portuguese soup recipes; or the latest accomplishments of her beautiful and talented songstress, songwriter daughter Karen Jones. Ellie says, "Each week people come to say hello to me while I am sitting on the porch waiting for the second service to begin. They greet me with a kiss, sit down, drink coffee, and exchange some laughs and tears from the previous week. Some weeks we try to solve all of the problems of the world, but we don't worry because we always have each other to talk to next week."

Elinor Jones was born in 1929 at the beginning of the Great Depression. She was the grandchild of immigrants from the Azores Islands and the Cape Verde Islands. In this country, her grandparents had what we would consider a mixed marriage. "My grandfather was from Cape Verde. Cape Verde is off the coast of North Africa and its people are considered black Africans. My grandmother was from the Azores, where she was considered white. They married in their teens and had four children. Their parents and families turned away from each of them for marrying outside of the race. They had a boy and three girls. My mother was the second daughter. Neither one of them was educated, so they struggled. My grandfather worked in the cotton mills, and as the children came of age, they all took jobs in the cotton mills for eight to ten dollars a week to contribute to the family. They only had Sundays off, with no vacations and no medical benefits.

"My grandfather was a compulsive gambler and he would spend his paycheck before he got home on Friday night. So my grandmother stayed home and managed the family and the money. She went to my grandfather's boss and explained the situation and they agreed that she would pick up his paycheck every Friday night. Out of necessity, my grandmother was a Strong Black Woman. She held the family together, kept food on the table and a roof over our heads. We were all expected to contribute to the family, and we all knew right from the beginning our positions in the family. Most importantly, we knew that the family would only prosper if everyone pulled together.

"As the kids got older, they got married and had their own families. My mother got married and had my brother and me; however, she got a divorce from my father when I was a baby. So, I grew up not knowing my father that well. My mother never said anything bad about my father. She let us form our own opinion about him. My mother, brother, and I moved back in with my grandparents. So while I didn't know my father that well, I had my grandfather and my brother in the house.

"When the Great Depression hit, everybody lost their jobs. Having a job meant that everybody contributed to the well being of the whole. While we didn't have jobs, everybody still had to help out in any way we could. We went on welfare like a lot of the poor people, but we never felt poor. As a matter of fact, my mother used to have a can that we would put pennies in for the poor. Even though we were poor, we gave those pennies to those less fortunate than we were. We had each other, and my mother never let us think that being poor was something to be sad about or ashamed of. Now, she did have this thing about cleanliness. For her it was a matter of self-respect to keep a clean home and body. She prided herself on being able to eat off our floors and she would not accept anyone who did not keep a clean home and body. It didn't matter to her how old or tattered your clothes were, as long as they were clean.

She used to say that soap and water were still the cheapest things out there, so there was no excuse to let yourself go.

"In my family, you didn't get too much praise for what you did, but you knew you were loved by the special acts of care you received. My mother and grandparents showed their love by the delicious and healthy meals they prepared. Growing up in a cold-water flat, the only room with heat was the kitchen with its black coal stove. I went to sleep many nights when it was so cold I could see the steam coming out of my mouth. We would get dressed and undressed under the covers because it was so cold. My grandfather would iron our sheets each night so we wouldn't get into a cold bed. This was just one of the many simple ways our parents and grandparents showed us how much we were loved.

"When I was seventeen years old, my mother met a new man and decided to marry. I wanted her to have some happiness in her life, so I moved out on my own and took several jobs as a live-in housekeeper. I worked for private families and lived in very nice homes. This experience taught me to appreciate the humanity that we all share, regardless of race, creed, or color. It taught me that without open and honest dialogue and respect, we will never be able to move beyond our fear of difference. These years were a very free time of my life. I always kept an open mind and tried to have as many positive experiences as I could. I even worked as a nude model for an art school. Hey, I figured, while I had this body, why not show it off? Actually, that was more boring work than you might think.

"Since I was a young girl, I have always loved books, history, and music. I used to get up at midnight to listen to Cab Calloway on the radio. My mother and I used to go to the jazz clubs together so I could listen to the music. We would both listen to the music and drink Coca-Cola.

"My mother always taught us to stay in touch with our feelings and to use common sense. She wanted us to understand that everybody had their own truth that they live by. She said that I had to develop my own truth, which is why she never took us to church. She did, however, teach us to live by the golden rule: do unto others as you would have them do unto you. She believed in loving your fellow human being, and in always conducting yourself in public with self-respect. I wouldn't realize until I became seriously ill just how spiritual my mother and grandmother really were.

"On Fathers Day in 1948, my father died. Two weeks later, I received a call that my mother, who had recently remarried and was living in Nantucket, had been diagnosed with cancer that had spread throughout her body. The doctors said that they had done all they could do for my mother. She was not expected to last much longer. These were tough days for me. All I had to rely upon was the love and laughter that had come to mean so much in my life. Through this difficult time in my life, I learned the meaning of surrender. Mom passed away just a year and a half after she had found a new husband, a new life, and a new love. That was a hard pill for me to swallow.

"After my mother and father died, it was time for me to leave my hometown, so I moved to Cleveland, continued doing live-in housekeeping work, and became more involved with music and musicians. The guys loved to keep me around because I made them laugh. I have always loved to laugh and see others laugh. When I laugh I feel free inside. I have been told that I know how to tell a good joke, too. When you laugh, you chase people who are afraid to laugh away. But after three years of living the club life, I began to see that I couldn't really do this much longer because it was an empty life.

"I moved from Cleveland and took a job with a wonderful family in Chicago. While I lived there, I came across a book called *The Prophet* by Kahlil Gibran. That book really moved me. Also during this time, I became very ill and was hospitalized. While I was in the hospital one night and in a lot of pain, I remember being held by a woman's arm covered in a black shawl with fringe. The feeling was so warm that all my pain went away and I fell off to sleep. The next day I asked the doctors who had come to visit me last night and they said I didn't have any visitors. I called my grandmother and told her what happened and she told me not to worry because that woman was her mother, my great-grandmother. This experience was so real that it started my exploration into my spirituality. I learned that love is a powerful force that stays with us long after we leave our bodies.

"While living in Chicago, I returned to Cleveland to visit a friend. During that weekend I met Eddie Jones, the man who would eventually become my husband. Eddie was a tall, dark, and handsome bass player who played with Count Basie during the swing period. We married and had two girls, Kathy and Karen. Life was full and hectic. I was busy being a homemaker. Money was tight, and eventually Eddie left his music to take a job with IBM. He became a workaholic, we stopped communicating, and before I knew it we had grown apart. Eddie never knew how to express his feelings, and that only got worse when our oldest daughter Kathy became ill and died of congenital heart failure. I thought that Kathy's death might bring us closer together, but we didn't know how to reach each other emotionally. I went into a very deep depression for a year and I had to get help. But we weren't there for each other emotionally. I lost my laugh during this time. I though I was losing my mind. These were very dark days."

Reclaiming Her Joy

MISS ELLIE'S MARRIAGE EVENTUALLY ENDED IN DIVORCE. WHILE that was many years ago, Miss Ellie has moved forward to create a wonderful life for herself and a loving relationship with her daughter Karen. Today, at the vital age of seventy-five, Ellie looks back on life and shared with me an entry she posted in her journal from a New Age author named Lazarus. In it, Lazarus wrote about the importance of willingness in creating what you desire in life: "The new age is an age of humanity, an age of consciousness, in which each individual willingly and enthusiastically accepts personal responsibility for consciously creating reality. Willingness, we would suggest, is an important part of this responsible reality creation. Begin a powerful personal journey using choice and decision, thought and feelings, and attitude and belief as the raw materials of change."

After reading to me from her journal, Ellie had the following to say about reclaiming joy and laughter in her life. I thought her words were the perfect way to conclude what this book has to say about the challenges facing Strong Black Women in their efforts to step out from behind the myths surrounding their lives, and to achieve new levels of self-care, peace of mind, and joy in their lives: "During these days I had to reclaim what I had lost in myself. What I had lost in my life was gone forever, but what I had lost in myself, I could reclaim. Life is always going to present us with struggle. Struggle is a spiritual test to see if you are willing to take total responsibility for your joy. Only you can hold onto the love you have for yourself and for others. If you let it slip away, or fail to claim it as your own, it is like missing the punch line of a really funny joke. Today, I tell jokes, read, listen to music, spend time with close friends, and most of all I laugh and hopefully inspire others—to enjoy each day to the fullest."

Love Is the Greatest Strength of All

LOVE HEALS. ABSOLUTE LOVE HEALS ABSOLUTELY. WHAT ELINOR Jones and many of the Strong Black Women that I have met during the writing of this book have taught me is the incorruptible healing power of love. There is a just and upright nature to abiding love that is stronger than myth, stereotype, lies, and pain. In many of the life stories of the women I interviewed for this book, the reclamation of joy came through the recognition and honor of love as the driving force in their lives. As my dear friend Diane says, "To love me, I gotta do me." It starts with the self-love that we show through the self-care we give ourselves. Through self-love and self-care, we inform and instruct those who are in our lives that we will only accept their loving thoughts and actions in return. In doing so, we form the basis for stepping into each day in a manner that enables us to respond to the day's struggles without sacrificing self-love.

True self-help starts with questions, not answers. So rather than leave you with some rules, steps, or laws to follow, I want to offer you five questions for joyful living that you should examine and live through each day of your life as a practice of supporting your intention of making peace with your life.

1. What can I do today to show the world that I love me?

   When was the last time you took a mental health day, treated yourself to a foot massage, told the kids that it was your turn to watch your favorite prime-time television program, chose a heart-healthy selection from the lunch menu, brought fresh flowers for your desk, took a walk through the park after dinner, or just slept late in bed on Saturday morning? Each day is a clean slate, and as such, you must create new opportunities for love and self-care. Thinking in advance of what you can do to announce to the world that you are committed to your joy will set the day up in your favor.

2. What can I do to simply let fear, pain, anger, or sorrow pass through my day?

   Be very aware of what you hold on to. Most people, places, events, and things are merely passing through our lives. How long will you allow yourself to hold a grudge today? Are you still upset about something someone said to you last week? Have you decided to avoid a particular establishment because the last time you went there you had a negative experience? Most of what causes us to sacrifice our joy and inner peace has nothing to do with what is happening in this exact moment of our lives. By simply letting events of fear, pain, anger, and sorrow pass through your day, you reserve that space for positive energy. Love cancels out fear, pain, anger, and sorrow, if you call upon it as a response to unfortunate circumstances.

3. Where is the most peaceful place in my life today, and how much time will I set aside to spend there?

   Will taking an extra five minutes in the shower to let the water just gently massage your body start your day off on a positive note? Can you close the office door and take a catnap during lunch? How about driving to work while listening to your favorite CD instead of clearing your office-phone mailbox from your cell phone? Is there a chapel near your office that offers a lunchtime prayer session? Finding a place and time to spend in communion with your loving thoughts and feelings can restore your spirit.

4. What do I need to do today to laugh out loud?

Do you have a friend who tells great jokes? Do you read the comic strips? Can you find something funny about the events of your day today? Do you take your life-roles too seriously? We have numerous opportunities to laugh at life every day, but we don't always take advantage of them. I like to keep a picture of my dogs on my computer, which makes me smile (and sometimes laugh out loud) when I think about some of the crazy and annoying things they have done over the years. Laughter is a healing art that is free to all who appreciate its form. If nothing else works, just try tickling yourself.

5. How do I want to be remembered by the lives I touch today?

We are all memorable for reasons that we don't even realize. We can also dictate how we are remembered by the people we interact with each day. Do you remember the stranger who held the door open for you as you ran for the bus this morning? Even if you don't remember that person, his humanity will stand out in your mind for the remainder of the day. What do you want people to remember about your humanity just for today?

I hope that these five questions for daily living help you to transcend the myths of strength in your life and to reclaim the love, self-care, and joy that is divinely yours to embrace.

AFFIRMATION

Today I am great, approaching wonderful,
and headed for joy!

ACKNOWLEDGEMENTS

IN WRITING THIS BOOK, I WAS REMINDED OF THE COMMUNITY OF people over the years who have led me to this very moment, and I am grateful to all of them for the contributions they have made both to my life and to the creation of this book. They are the source of my strength.

First, I would like to thank my publisher, Doug Seibold of Agate, for believing in me and this project, and also the entire wonderful team at Agate.

Eric Myers, my dear friend and agent, and the whole Spieler Agency, thanks for your warmth, sensitivity, and savvy business acumen. You believed in this project from the very beginning and for that I am grateful.

I would also like to thank my friend and ghost editor Melissa Moonves for your support, enthusiasm, and invaluable contribution to making this book an instrument of healing. I look forward to working with you on many more projects over the years.

Leslie Brown, Eddie Padilla, Julie Brumlik, Rosie Gordon Wallace, and my dear Wildebrando Pichardo, you all have been the foundation for my creative process and my serenity. Thank you for your unconditional love and support during the most difficult times in this journey.

There is a village of friends and loved ones without whom I would have never been able to endure a post-9/11 New York while writing a book about love, self-care, and joy. I will never forget all that you have done for me. They include Rodney Cotton, John Hamilton, Ted Stewart, Ed Robinson, Scott Albert, Kevin Hopkins, Sandra Nichols, Maritzio Martinoli, Diaspora Vibe Gallery and the Diaspora Vibe Cultural Arts Incubator, Lenny Stephens, Dwina Gibb, Robert Oliver, Kerry Lattanzio and "Dante," Roland Newport, Samuel Autman, Susan Shapiro, Linda Duiggans, Cavakia Therlonge, Noelia Orta, Dr. Izzy Maldonado, Marlon Hill Esq., Patti Johnson, Tomas Leal, Jose Cox, Mary Harlan, Shawne Johnson, Diane Smith, Linda Eckhardt, bell hooks, Jesus Salguiero, Marc Livingston, Milca Esdaille, Darnella Cordier, Gloria Burnett, Olga Edridge, Yvonne Mobley, Earthlyn Manuel, Miriam Gonzalzles, Hasam Akbar, and Michael Herrod of Great Adventure Travel in Miami, Florida.

Thank you to the following people who in their own special ways have taught me that paradise lives within each of us: Reverend Jeremiah T. Wright, Reverend Bill Cameron, Reverend James Trapp of Unity on the Bay in Miami, and the Brahama Kumaris.

A special and heartfelt thank-you to Cynthia Wilson.

To my muse and dear friend Paul Rogers, thanks for always challenging me to be the adventurer.

A big hug and endless gratitude to Shari Higman, Denny Guerra, and the folks at Canine Country Club in Miami for caring for my dogs Seal and Nana while I ran this race to becoming a writer.

I also want to thank a few of the mentors throughout my career as a diversity consultant who challenged me to express my creative voice and individuality: Bea Young, Will Lucas, John Kirksey, Joyce Dudley, and Muriel Lazar.

To my family, I love you all—Bessie, Roger, Lisa, Derek, Collina, Onna, Kenny, Junnie, Edna, Bill, Pam, Pat, Grace Martin, Carlton Williams, and all the other members of my tribe.

Finally, I would like to thank the folks at the Harlem Book Fair and the Countee Cullen Branch of the New York Public Library.